Bank Finance

BANK FINANCE

Brian Coyle

FINANCIAL
WORLD
Publishing
THE CHARTERED INSTITUTE OF BANKERS

Financial World Publishing
IFS House
4-9 Burgate Lane
Canterbury
Kent
CT1 2XJ
United Kingdom

Telephone: 01227 818687

Financial World Publishing publications are published by
The Chartered Institute of Bankers, a non-profit making registered educational charity.

Typeset by Kevin O'Connor
Printed in Italy

ISBN 0-85297-458-2

Contents

Introduction

Banks and their customers have differing perceptions of bank lending. To most bankers, lending is not a capital-market activity, and yet to many corporate customers, particularly small and medium-sized companies, bank loans are their most important external source of capital. The use of the capital markets by companies to raise debt or equity cannot be appreciated properly without understanding the significance of bank lending as a key source of long-term funding.

Commercial Banking and Investment Banking

Banking services can be divided into two broad categories, commercial banking and investment banking or merchant banking.

Commercial banking consists mainly of money-transmission services, the management of customer bank accounts and deposits, and lending. Bank loans are a commercial-banking product.

Investment banking consists of specialist financial services and securities-market activities. In the securities markets, an investment bank acts as an intermediary, helping an issuer of securities to obtain funds from other investors, rather than lending the bank's own funds.

In the US, the Banking Act of 1933, known as the Glass-Steagall Act, prohibited commercial banks from involvement in securities trading and underwriting either directly or through a subsidiary company. The purpose of the act was to protect commercial banking against the risks of investment losses from securities-market trading. This in turn was intended to protect customers' bank deposits against the risk of financial collapse of their bank. As a consequence US banks at one time were either commercial banks or investment banks.

More recently, the Glass-Steagall Act has been interpreted less strictly, and some commercial banks carry out some investment-banking activities. Even so, the distinction between commercial banking and investment banking is still clear-cut, and bank lending is a commercial banking rather than a capital-market activity.

Bank Loans and Facilities as Capital

The demand for medium-term or long-term lending comes mainly from commercial and industrial companies, and from private individuals. Banks and central governments normally do not need to raise long-term money by means of bank loans.

- Most inter-bank borrowing and lending is short term, and is regarded as a money market activity.
- Banks wishing to borrow long-term usually will do so by issuing debt securities.
- A central government borrows by issuing securities or by encouraging government-run savings schemes for private individuals.

Because banks and central governments do not use bank loans for long-term funding, they do not consider bank loans as a capital-market activity.

Banks and their corporate customers can have differing attitudes towards the permanence of bank funding. Many bank-lending facilities are either short-term or uncommitted. Uncommitted overdraft facilities to a customer, for example, can be reduced by the bank without notice. To the banks, these facilities are short-term.

In contrast, companies that rely on bank loans and facilities as a source of finance could regard them as quasi-permanent capital. To the corporate borrower, if bank finance is going to be needed for the foreseeable future, it can make sense to think of these funds as part of its long-term financial structure. Overdraft facilities can be renewed, and maturing short-term loans replaced by new loans.

Bank Lending and Risk Management

Bank lending creates risks for both the borrower and the lender.

The financial risks for the borrower arise from the consequences of:

- being unable to obtain loan finance when it is needed
- being unable to pay interest and repay the loan principal in full and on time
- restrictive loan covenants that prevent the borrower from obtaining further loan finance when extra funding is required.

A corporate borrower should be able to negotiate suitable loan terms from its bank(s), and also ensure that the banks will be supportive should the company run into difficulties with its loan payments.

Running a Loan Book

A bank must decide what assets to hold and what liabilities to use to fund them. In establishing a lending portfolio or loan book, there are three major risks to consider:

- credit risk – the risk that borrowers will fail to pay what they owe
- liquidity risk – the risk that the bank will have insufficient cash income from its assets to meet the payment obligations on its liabilities when they fall due
- interest-rate risk – the risk of an adverse movement in interest rates affecting the bank's profits; for example, for a bank that

makes fixed-rate loans funded by variable-rate liabilities, the risk of a rise in market interest rates.

A bank's objective should be to maximize its profits from lending subject to the need to keep these risks under control and at an acceptable level.

The main risk for a lending bank is credit risk. This can be controlled, and kept within acceptable limits, by tight credit management, and by:

- agreeing to lend only to companies whose creditworthiness has been checked and judged to be satisfactory
- taking security for the loan, or a guarantee
- imposing conditions on the loan such as loan covenants that the customer must keep to avoid being in default
- monitoring the interest payments and principal repayments, and taking action whenever payments are overdue.

For banks, liquidity risk and interest-rate risk can be controlled by matching the maturities of assets and liabilities, for example by funding six-month loans out of six-month deposits. To some extent, especially in the eurocurrency lending market, this is what banks do.

The Importance of Banks to Corporate Activity

Banks are one of the most important suppliers to companies. Even if a company is strongly cash positive, and therefore does not require bank finance, it will require commercial banking services such as current accounts, supplier payment facilities, including cheques, electronic funds transfers, credit-card arrangements, and so on. In addition, if it operates internationally, it will require foreign-exchange conversion and hedging facilities. Most companies do require bank finance that raises the status of the company's bank or banks to one of major supplier. Without the raw material of finance, these companies could not function.

Purpose of this Book

The purpose of this book is to describe various aspects of bank finance. From a borrowing-company's point of view, it is important to know how loans and facilities can be structured, and what their features could be. It is important to understand a bank's lending strategy because this could determine its response to a customer's request to borrow.

In the loan-negotiation process, the bank and the borrower must look after their own interests. They also should recognize the other's requirements and concerns, because in reaching a loan agreement there can be some give and take. Banking relationships, and the aftercare of lending, also can be important for a borrower, to secure long-term access to bank finance as a source of funds.

Structuring Bank Finance

Before the second half of the twentieth century, bank lending to companies consisted almost entirely of overdraft finance. Any cash deficit was financed by the company's bank on a day-to-day basis by means of a rolling overdraft. A deficit could be funded in this way for months, or possibly years. Technically a bank could request repayment of the overdraft at any time, but usually the lending could be renewed daily for an extended period so that the finance had the status, but not the structure, of a long-term loan.

The lending markets have evolved and banks now offer a range of different funding structures to accommodate the needs of the corporate borrower.

Features of Loan Finance

Elements in the structuring of a bank loan or facility are:

- the term of the loan or facility
- the interest-rate basis
- pricing structure
- whether the funding should be provided as a loan or facility
- the repayment profile
- security and guarantees
- covenants
- representations and warranties
- the currency of borrowing.

A loan may be bilateral, between one bank and the borrower, but large loans may be syndicated between a number of banks.

Term of Loan

Banks will lend money to companies for periods of as short as one day, and as long as ten years. In certain circumstances they will lend for as long as 15 or 20 years, but such instances are rare and are better catered for by the bond markets.

Although banks are prepared to lend funds for periods as short as one day and as long as ten years, they do have preferences. Generally speaking, they are reluctant to lend beyond five years, even to high-quality corporate customers. This is because the perceived credit risk increases with the term of the loan. A bank might apply its own internal risk-weighting rules, giving a higher risk weighting to loans in excess of five years, and having a policy of no lending to companies in excess of a given term except in special circumstances. Banks that are prepared to lend beyond five years may insist on charging a variable rate of interest, to avoid an exposure to interest-rate risk.

Interest-Rate Basis: Fixed or Variable Rate

The rate of interest applicable to a loan can be either a fixed or floating rate.

Fixed-rate loans have the interest rate fixed at the outset for the full term of the loan. One benchmark for setting fixed-rate interest on corporate loans is the rate of interest being paid on government securities of a similar term to maturity. Government securities should be low-risk; therefore fixed-rate corporate loans with the same term to maturity will carry a higher rate of interest. For example, if the market rate of interest on fixed-rate government bonds with five years to maturity is 5%, the fixed rate on a five-year loan to a large creditworthy company might be 6.5%, 150 basis points above the risk-free government-bond rate. Other useful benchmark interest rates for fixed-term lending are the rates of interest available in the interest-rate swaps market for swaps of different terms.

Banks usually are unwilling to lend at a fixed rate to small corporate borrowers, except for fairly short-term lending of up to two years.

Interest-rate (coupon) swaps give large borrowers the flexibility to switch from fixed-rate to variable-rate payments or vice versa. For large creditworthy borrowers, the general preference of banks for floating-rate over fixed-rate lending is not a serious problem.

The interest rate payable on floating-rate loans is reset at regular intervals throughout the loan term by reference to a benchmark rate of interest. The new interest rate from each reset or rollover date applies until the next reset date. Floating-rate loans can be reset as often as daily. It is normal for borrowers to be given a choice of reset period when the loan is negotiated. Most corporates opt for quarterly, semi-annual or annual reset dates because more frequent changes could become an administrative burden for those responsible for monitoring.

The rate of interest on variable-rate loans will be at a margin above a reference or benchmark rate of interest.

Pricing Structure

There are two main pricing elements for a bank loan:

- an arrangement fee, and
- an interest rate (drawing rate).

There is a supplementary element of price for a standby bank facility known as a commitment fee. In addition, the borrower normally pays legal fees for its own and the bank's advisers.

Arrangement Fee

An arrangement fee is a one-off upfront fee payable to the bank in compensation for:

- considering the company's loan application
- assessing the company's creditworthiness
- negotiating the loan
- if the loan is syndicated, assembling the participating banks into a syndicate.

An arrangement fee for a loan can be as low as ten basis points (0.10%) of the loan principal or the amount of the facility. Small-business loans and personal loans can involve arrangement fees of 100 to 150 basis points or even more in some cases. An arrangement fee also is payable when loans or facilities are refinanced or extended at the end of their original term.

Different names can be given to arrangement fees. A management fee, for example, would be payable to underwriters of a syndicated facility, and an agency fee to the lead bank. (Syndicated facilities are explained in Chapter 5.)

Drawing Rate

The drawing rate is the loan interest rate, if and when the money is drawn, under an overdraft facility or revolving credit facility. Floating-rate loans or bank facilities normally are priced at an agreed margin over the prevailing market rate of interest at the time of drawing the loan (drawdown) or at the rollover or reset date – when one interest period ends and another begins.

The full amount of a fixed-rate loan is borrowed at the outset. These loans are priced at a rate of interest that reflects market rates of interest at the time of the negotiations. Acceptance of a fixed-rate offer normally will be binding on the company.

Commitment Fee or Facility Fee

A standby facility involves a bank promising to lend up to an agreed amount, should the customer wish to borrow. A commitment fee for a standby facility compensates the bank for undertaking to provide funds upon demand. A commitment fee normally is expressed as a percentage amount, payable per annum, on the undrawn portion of the facility.

Example
A $10 million facility is subject to a commitment fee of 25 basis points per annum. The facility was 50% drawn during a particular year.

Analysis
The commitment fee for the year will be $12,500
($10 million x 50% x 0.25%).

Banks sometimes ask for a facility fee rather than a commitment fee. The difference is that a facility fee is payable on the full amount of the facility, whether or not it is drawn. In the example above, the annual payment under a facility fee of 25 basis points per annum would be $25,000 ($10 million x 0.25%).

Other Pricing Features
In addition to the fees described above, a loan agreement could include additional pricing features that the banks use either to enhance their return or to regulate the use of a facility by the customer. For example, the cost of a standby facility could include a utilization margin, whereby the customer must pay more for using the facility extensively. For example any drawings in excess of 50% of the total amount of a facility could be subject to a step-up in interest rate. A step-up in interest rates for variable-rate borrowing is achieved by charging a higher margin over LIBOR or base rate, for example by raising the interest charged from 150 basis points over LIBOR to 175 basis points over LIBOR. The purpose of a step-up provision in a loan agreement would be to deter the borrower from drawing excessively on the facility.

Legal/Documentation Fees
Unless the loan agreement is a standard agreement, preparing the formal

loan contract often calls for the services of two sets of lawyers, one to represent the bank and one for the customer. The bank sometimes will insist on a customer using external rather than inhouse lawyers, and many banks favor the use of external lawyers to represent their own interest in the transaction. The borrower must pay for both sets of lawyers. Because of the potentially high cost of legal fees, and the elaborate detail in many legal agreements for high-value loans, these costs can be high.

A simple term loan or an overdraft facility agreement for fairly small amounts of money ideally might be subject to a full examination by a lawyer acting for the borrower. However, given the limited financial resources of a small company, normally it is sufficient for the company's representative to understand the terms and conditions in the agreement, and to rely on the bank's assurance that the terms are standard for most small borrowers.

All-in Cost of Borrowing

To calculate the all-in cost of funds for a borrowing transaction, front-end fees should be amortized over the life of the loan. The shorter the term of the loan, the greater is the impact of one-off fees on the overall borrowing cost.

Example

Beta Inc. wishes to borrow $1,000,000 for two years. The legal cost of drawing up the loan agreement would be $15,000 and the bank would levy an arrangement fee of 100 basis points. Interest would be fixed for the two-year period at 7.5% per annum.

Analysis

The full cost of the loan would be:

	$	**% per annum**
Interest ($75,000 per annum)	150,000	7.50
Arrangement fee	10,000	0.50
Legal costs	15,000	0.75
	175,000	8.75

If the same loan had been for a term of just six months, with the same arrangement fee and legal costs, the annual equivalent of the full interest cost would have been as follows:

	$	% per annum
Interest (6 months)	37,500	7.5
Arrangement fee	10,000	2.0
Legal costs	15,000	3.0
	62,500	12.5

Other Aspects of Bank Finance

Other features of the structuring bank finance are dealt with in following chapters.

Repayment Profile

The repayment profile of a loan refers to the way in which the loan principal will be repaid. The loan principal might be repaid in full at maturity, or gradually over the term of the loan. Interest is payable on the amount of loan principal outstanding, i.e. the amount of the loan that has not yet been repaid. Three types of repayment profile are:

- bullet
- balloon, and
- amortizing.

Bullet Repayment

Bullet repayment requires the loan principal to be repaid in a single lump sum at the end of the term of the loan. For example, if a five-year loan of $200,000 at 5% interest per annum has a bullet repayment profile, the loan principal outstanding will be the full $200,000 at the end of the loan period, as illustrated in the diagram opposite.

Bullet Repayment

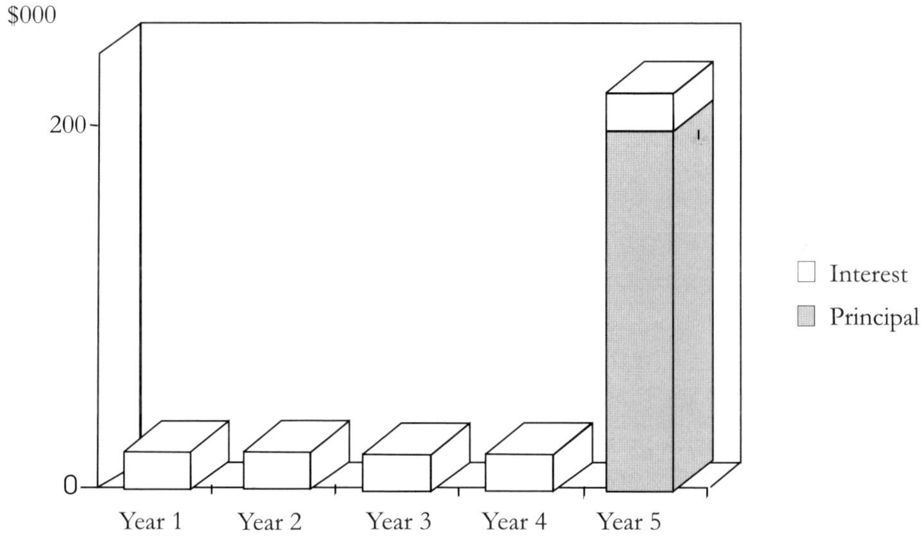

Balloon Repayment

A balloon repayment requires some of the loan principal to be repaid during the term of the loan. At maturity there is still a substantial proportion of loan principal outstanding that is then repaid.

For example, suppose a company obtains a five-year loan of $200,000. Loan payments are annual, each payment consisting of interest plus a capital repayment of $20,000 in each of the first four years, and the balance of the loan principal repaid at the end of the loan term.

There will be four annual principal repayments of $20,000, or $80,000 in total in the first four years, leaving $120,000 still to be paid when the loan period ends. This is then paid in full. This balloon repayment profile is illustrated in the diagram below.

Balloon Repayment

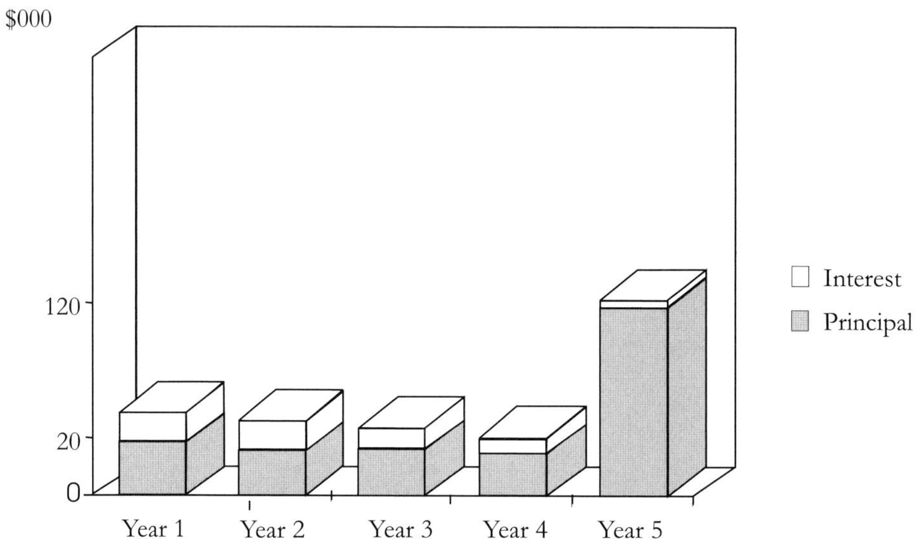

Amortizing Loan

The loan principal of an amortizing loan is repaid gradually over the term of the loan. Loan payments at regular intervals, usually every month, quarter or six months, consist of interest and a repayment of some of the principal. At the final loan payment, the principal outstanding falls to zero. Mortgage repayment loans operate in this way.

Example
A company borrows $193,050 for five years at a fixed-interest rate of 10%, with six-monthly loan payments. A fixed rate of 10% per annum is here taken to mean a fixed rate of 5% interest each six months. It is a normal amortizing loan, and all the six-monthly payments are for the same amount. The loan will be repaid in ten amounts of $25,000 each. Each payment will consist partly of interest and partly of loan principal repayment. The interest element is the loan principal outstanding at the start of the six-month period multiplied by an interest rate of 5% for the six months. The loan principal repayment is the difference between the total payment and the interest element. As the interest element declines,

the loan principal element increases. The repayment profile is shown in the table below. There is a rounding error of $. Allowing for this, the loan principal is repaid in full with the final loan payment of $25,000 at the end of the fifth year.

Payment date	**Loan payment**	**Interest element**	**Principal repayment**	**Loan principal outstanding**
	$	**$**	**$**	**$**
Start of loan, Year 1	-	-	-	193,050
Month 6, Year 1	25,000	9,652	15,348	177,702
Month 12, Year 1	25,000	8,885	16,115	161,587
Month 6, Year 2	25,000	8,079	16,921	144,666
Month 12, Year 2	25,000	7,233	17,767	126,899
Month 6, Year 3	25,000	6,344	18,656	108,243
Month 12, Year 3	25,000	5,412	19,588	88,655
Month 6, Year 4	25,000	4,432	20,568	68,087
Month 12, Year 4	25,000	3,404	21,596	46,491
Month 6, Year 5	25,000	2,324	22,676	23,815
Month 12, Year 5	25,000	1,191	23,809	6

Notes on these calculations:

1. The loan repayments are all £25,000.
2. The interest element in the loan is 5% of the amount outstanding on the loan at the end of the previous interest period.

3. The principal repayment is the difference between the $25,000 of the loan payment and the interest element in the payment. This is subtracted from the loan principal still outstanding at the start of the period to obtain the loan outstanding at the end of the period.

This amortization repayment profile is illustrated below:

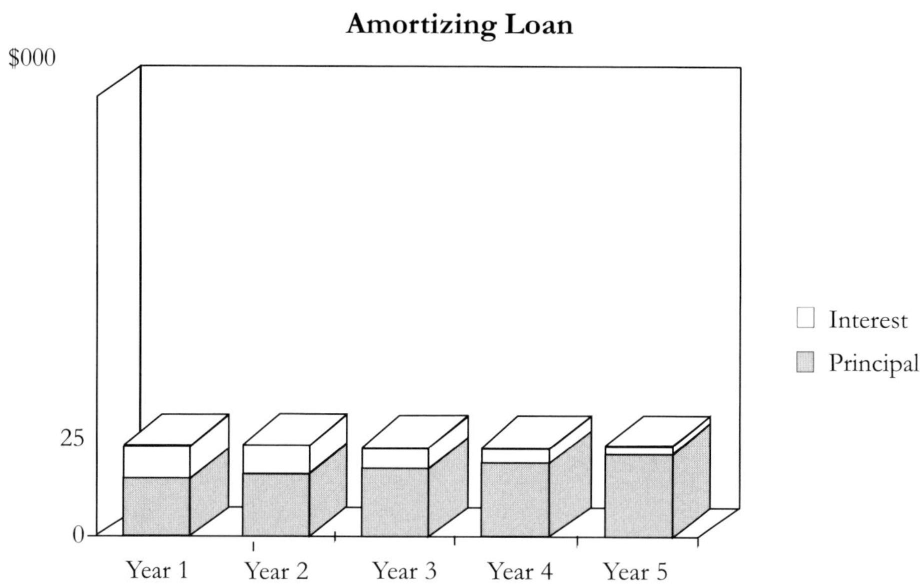

Equal Amortizing Loan

An equal amortizing loan is one in which the principal is repaid in equal installments. Interest is paid on the loan principal outstanding; therefore the borrower's payments of principal and interest decline with each payment over the term of the loan. The principal repayment is a constant amount; however the interest payable is less with each subsequent payment because of the lower amount of loan principal outstanding. This is illustrated opposite for a five-year equal amortizing loan of $100,000.

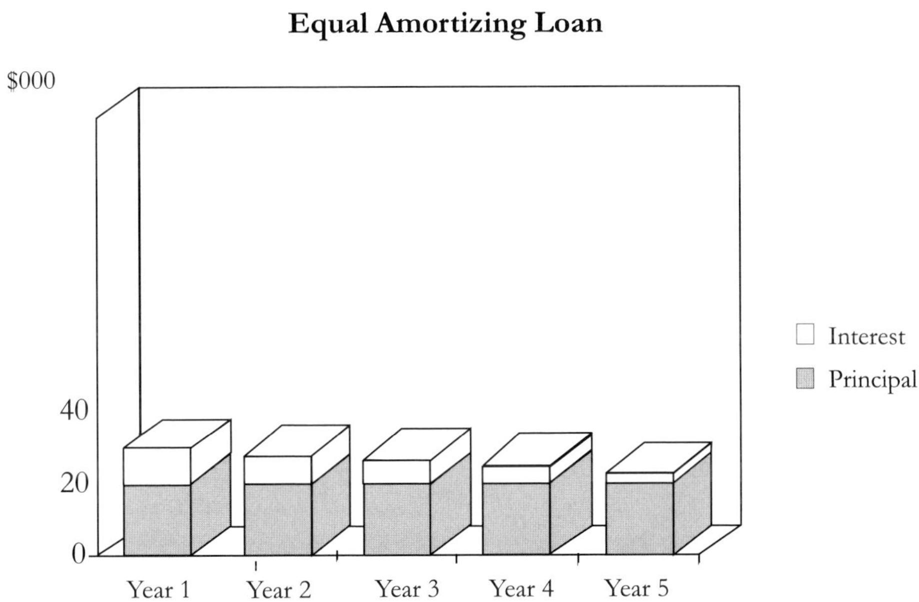

Alternative Repayment Profiles

There are other variations in repayment profiles.

- The repayment schedule can be structured to fit precisely the income generation of the project or business that is being funded by the loan. This can involve a repayment schedule with a *holiday period*, particularly during the early years of the loan, so that regular repayments of principal do not commence until the project reaches its cash-generation phase.
- The principal repayments can be tailored to fit an irregular pattern of project payback. This is known as *sawtooth-repayment* schedule or *roller-coaster* loan because the outstanding loan principal can go up and down during the loan term.
- On occasion, a bank could agree to receive interest for a time at less than its required rate so that the total loan principal increases. For example, a loan could be arranged for which the

bank wants 9% interest but receives 7%. The 2% difference is added to the loan principal. If there is a bullet repayment the total repayment at maturity will exceed the amount of the initial loan. This is an *accreting loan*.

Selecting the Repayment Profile

A company should try to structure its repayment obligations under a loan agreement to suit the expected cash flows of the project that is being funded or of the company as a whole. To some extent banks are indifferent as to whether a loan is repaid in instalments or in a bullet repayment at the maturity date. However, given a choice, banks might prefer repayment by instalments because this reduces the amount of their credit exposure to the borrower progressively during the loan term. An amortizing loan is a lower credit risk for a bank than a loan with bullet repayment, and in view of this lower risk, the loan might be priced at a lower rate of interest than for a comparable bullet loan.

Loans and Facilities

Matching the Loan or Facility to the Borrower's Needs

A loan facility should be arranged to meet the requirements of the borrower. There are different types of loan facility, each designed to meet different customer requirements and circumstances. Important factors in deciding what type of facility might be most appropriate are:

- What is the loan facility for? Why does the borrower want the money?
- How does the borrower expect to repay the loan capital? Where is the money going to come from to make the repayment?
- Is it important that the funds should be committed so that the bank will be unable to call in the loan on demand?

Finance for Day-to-Day Operating Requirements

The borrower might want to borrow money to cover day-to-day cash deficits from trading operations. A typical trading company incurs operating expenditures, for example by purchasing stock and paying wages and salaries to employees. It also receives money from sales when its customers eventually pay what they owe. As a general rule, companies have to spend money before they earn it, and so might have short-term cash shortages, especially when the business is growing. It might need to borrow money to cover its short-term cash requirements, expecting to repay the loans out of its eventual operating income. The actual amount that the company needs to borrow should fluctuate with the patterns of cash receipts and payments from business operations.

Day-to-day cash requirements to cover short-term cash deficits traditionally have been financed by a *bank overdraft*. However, a bank also may be willing to provide a *term loan* for the same purpose.

Finance for Capital Expenditure

A company might have to borrow to finance a lump-sum expenditure, such as a capital expenditure on land and buildings, or plant and machinery. If so, it might need all the money at once. Alternatively, it might need some of the money now and some more later because the capital-expenditure program is scheduled over a period of several months or even several years.

Finance for capital expenditure often will be repaid out of the income eventually earned from the capital assets that are acquired. In such circumstances, the borrower might be willing to repay the loan principal gradually from its operating income. Each loan payment by the borrower will consist partly of interest and partly of some capital repayment. The outstanding amount of the loan will be reduced until it is fully paid off at the end of the loan period.

Alternatively, if returns from the capital spending will take some time to come in, the borrower might wish to defer repayment of the loan capital until the end of the loan term. The lending bank must be satisfied that the borrower will be able to make the repayment in this way.

Bank lending to finance capital expenditure normally is in the form of either:

- a *term loan*, when the loan money is provided in full at the start of the loan period, or
- a term loan, when the loan funds can be taken out at any time, for a period not exceeding the remaining duration of the loan facility and provided the maximum lending limit is not exceeded, or
- a *revolving credit facility*.

Types of Bilateral Loan or Facility

The most common types of bilateral loan facility are:

- an overdraft
- a term loan
- a revolving-credit facility.

Other types of loan facility include:

- an evergreen facility
- a standby facility
- a banker's acceptances (BA) arrangement.

Syndicated lending arrangements are described in Chapter 5.

Committed and Uncommitted Funds

A loan facility might be committed or uncommitted.

A committed facility means that the lending is prearranged, and can be accessed by the borrower:

- at any time, within the duration of the facility
- up to the maximum amount of the facility.

For example, if a bank overdraft facility for $5 million is committed up to 31 December Year 2, the borrower can run up an overdraft of up to $5 million at any time up to 31 December Year 2. The bank cannot reduce the borrowing limit or shorten the period of the lending facility because the facility is committed. In return for giving a commitment in advance, the bank will charge a commitment fee. Usually, a commitment fee is an annual charge for each year the facility is available.

If a facility is uncommitted, the bank is not obliged to advance further funds when the borrower asks for them. Instead, the bank has some discretion in deciding whether or not to lend extra money. The bank might even be able to call in money that already has been lent for immediate repayment, e.g. an uncommitted overdraft facility.

Overdraft Facility

An overdraft facility is a traditional method for a bank to finance the short-term borrowing requirements of individuals and companies. As a general rule, the understanding is that the overdraft will be repaid out of future operating income. A bank may offer a term loan instead of an overdraft, for the same purpose. Term loans and overdrafts might be offered for fairly long periods of several years, although overdraft facilities may be reviewed regularly.

The features of a bank overdraft facility include the following:

- A bank may agree to provide a company with a committed overdraft facility up to a stated amount, for a stated period of time.
- If a company draws on its account when there is an insufficient credit balance on the account, the bank will make the payment provided the overdraft limit is not exceeded as a result.
- The rate of interest payable on an arranged overdraft is subject to negotiation between the parties, and usually is set out in the overdraft facility letter to the customer. The rate of interest on an overdraft is quite high, and much higher than for a term loan.
- Interest is payable only on the overdraft balance, not on the total amount of the overdraft facility. A customer with an overdraft facility whose current account is in credit will not pay any interest so long as the account remains in credit.
- A customer may repay an overdraft without giving notice. This differs from a term loan where the customer may terminate the loan early, but usually only by giving notice to the bank.
- An overdraft facility may be committed for a specified period of time, but this is fairly unusual. An overdraft facility usually is uncommitted and repayable on demand.

Repayment on Demand

An overdraft is repayable on demand unless the bank has agreed otherwise with the customer. In other words, a facility is uncommitted unless the bank has agreed otherwise. This means that the bank can insist that the existing overdraft must be repaid in full, or reduced below a specified amount, whenever it wishes to do so.

The bank, in providing an uncommitted overdraft facility, will allow the customer to overdraw on his/her current account up to a certain maximum limit. This limit is negotiated between the bank and the customer, and may be altered during the period of the facility. In normal circumstances, even though the facility is uncommitted, the bank usually will allow the borrower to be overdrawn all the time, provided the size of the overdraft remains within the agreed limit.

In some circumstances, the bank may take action and insist that the borrower reduces the size of his/her overdraft. This is because the bank regards an overdraft as temporary finance for the borrower, to cover short-term cash deficits. An overdraft should not become permanent because it will in effect become a long-term loan. If a customer's overdraft continues to get bigger and the bank gets concerned about the prospects for repayment, it may demand immediate repayment. Some companies have gone into liquidation when a bank has demanded immediate repayment: this is a matter that a borrower should consider when negotiating an uncommitted facility.

Term Loans

A term loan is a loan of a specified amount, for a specified length of time (the term of the loan). Most term loans are for a period or maturity of up to five years, but depending on conditions in the banking industry, term loans may be offered to good customers for periods of up to ten years or even longer.

A term loan is usually a committed facility for the full term of a loan, and is not on demand. The bank cannot call in the loan whenever it wishes, unless the borrower is in default. The funds may be made available to the borrower:

- up front, in a single amount of money at the start of the loan term, or
- over an extended period of time, in several portions or tranches, as and when the borrower needs the money.

When the loan is provided in a single amount at the start of the loan term, the borrower usually will have a short period, the availability period, between the start of the agreement and the time by which the money will be available and has to be used. The repayment mehod is agreed between borrower and bank, and may be by bullet repayment, amortization, balloon repayment, etc.

A borrower may not repay the loan capital of a term loan and then borrow it back again. For example, suppose that a company borrows $100,000 for five years with amortization, and at the end of the third year, $35,000 of the loan capital has been repaid, leaving only $65,000 still to pay back. The borrower could not borrow a further $35,000 for two years, to bring the total amount borrowed back up to $100,000. In this respect, a term loan is different from a revolving credit facility.

Revolving Credit Facility

A revolving credit facility is a lending agreement whereby the bank makes available to the borrower a specified maximum amount of loan capital for a specified term.

- The borrower can draw down the loan capital in tranches, almost as and when required during the term of the facility.
- There is no agreed repayment schedule, and the borrower can repay the loan capital at any time. The loan capital must be repaid in full by the end of the term of the facility, and the total amount borrowed at any time cannot exceed the maximum limit of the facility.
- The borrower can repay some loan capital and then borrow more funds subsequently. In this respect, a revolving loan facility is different from a term loan.

- Interest is payable only on the loan capital outstanding, not on the full amount of the loans available under the facility.

A revolving credit facility usually is a committed facility, and the bank charges a commitment fee for providing it.

Example
It might clarify the nature of a revolving credit facility to show an illustrative example.

Suppose that a company arranges a two-year revolving credit facility for $25 million, from 1 January Year 1. The borrower might borrow in tranches and make capital repayments as follows. Note: Interest payments are ignored here.

Date	**Debt before the transaction**	**Draw down of funds**	**Repayment of funds**	**Debt after the transaction**
	$m	**$m**	**$m**	**$m**
10 January Year1	0	9.0		9.0
30 April Year 1	9.0	7.0		16.0
10 August Year1	16.0		5.0	11.0
1 Sept Year 1	11.0	12.0		23.0
10 January Year 2	23.0		9.0	14.0
29 March Year 2	14.0	5.0		19.0
30 April Year 2	19.0		7.0	12.0
31 Dec Year 2	12.0		12.0	0

During the period, the company has borrowed in excess of $30 million, but the total amount outstanding at any time never exceeds the $25 million limit of the facility.

Other Features of a Revolving-Credit-Facility Agreement
In some respects, a revolving-credit facility is similar to an overdraft because the amount borrowed at any time can rise and fall, provided it remains within the total permitted limit. However, there are important differences.

- The size of a revolving credit facility tends to be much larger than the size of an overdraft facility.
- Whereas an overdraft facility usually is provided to finance the borrower's working capital requirements, a revolving credit facility is more likely to be granted to allow the borrower to finance a capital expenditure program.
- A revolving credit facility allows for amounts of capital to be borrowed in portions or tranches. In contrast, an overdraft allows the amount borrowed to fluctuate according to cash receipts into the borrower's bank account and payments out of the account.
- Usually there is a minimum and a maximum permitted size for a tranche of borrowing.
- Each tranche is borrowed for a specific term, in the same way as a term loan. A borrower may draw down a tranche for three months or six months. The facility agreement might provide for a minimum loan period for each tranche of one month for example. At the maturity of a tranche of loan, the borrower doesn't have to repay the loan capital, Instead, the loan can be rolled over. In other words, the tranche of capital can be borrowed for a further period. Loans can be rolled over continually, if required, right up to the end of the credit facility.
- The facility agreement may provide for a maximum number of tranches of loan at any time. This would be to discourage the borrower from drawing down large numbers of tranches of the minimum amount, and so ease the administrative tasks for the bank in managing the loans.
- The total amount borrowed and still outstanding must be repaid when the facility comes to an end.

Other Types of Bilateral Loan Arrangement

Although overdrafts and term loans are the most common types of bilateral loan, other bilateral loan arrangements are worthy of mention.

Evergreen Facility

An evergreen facility is a term-loan agreement that includes a provision allowing the bank to extend the term of the loan beyond its original maturity, at the request of the borrower. For example, a term loan that originally was for a period of four years might be extended at the end of year 4 for a further three years beyond the end of year 4, i.e. to the end of year 7.

In theory, a loan with this provision could be extended repeatedly and indefinitely, and so be evergreen. Evergreen facilities are no longer common.

Standby Facility

A standby facility, as its name suggests, is a source of borrowing made available by a bank as a standby in the event that something goes wrong with the borrower's intended source of borrowing. It is a fall-back arrangement.

For example, a company might plan to raise finance by issuing medium-term notes (MTNs). In the event that the note issue fails to attract investors, and the company is unable to raise enough money by issuing them, its bank might provide a standby facility that it can draw on instead.

Banker's Acceptance (BA) Facility

A Banker's Acceptance facility (BA facility) is an arrangement covering a period of several years, typically two to five, during which a bank agrees, on behalf of a corporate customer, to accept bills of exchange that are drawn on it, up to a maximum limit.

An accepted bill of exchange is a promise to pay a specified amount at a future date, to the drawer of the bill. By accepting bills of exchange, the bank is giving its own promise to pay. Accepted bills can be sold before maturity in the discount market. Bank bills, i.e. bills accepted by banks, may attract a finer (lower) rate of discount.

A Banker's Acceptance facility can be used in two ways. Suppliers of the bank's customer, instead of seeking payment directly from the customer, can draw a bill on the bank. When the bank accepts it, the supplier's credit risk is with the bank, not the customer. This is illustrated below.

Banker's Acceptance

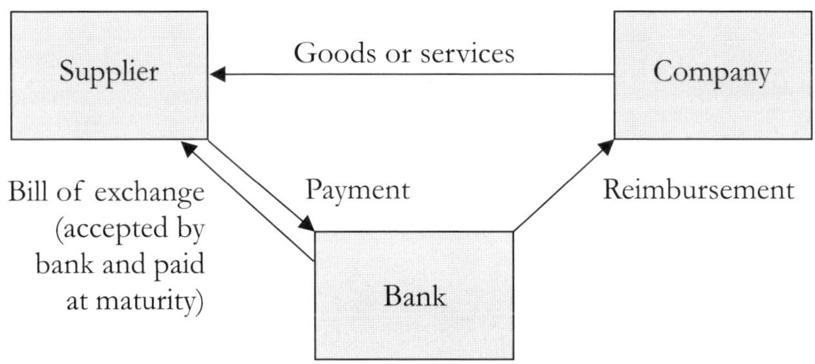

There is a second, and more common, use of a Banker's Acceptance facility. The customer, whenever it wishes to obtain short-term funds, can arrange to draw bills on the bank that the bank accepts. The customer can then sell these bills at fine rates in the discount market to raise funds. The bank is reimbursed by the company before the bills mature, i.e. before the bank has to pay the bill to the customer. The company can raise the funds to repay the bank by drawing further bills under the facility.

Banker's Acceptance

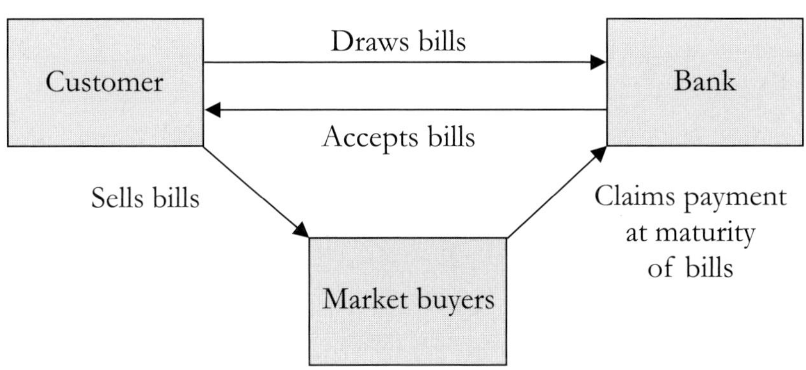

Summary

There are different types of bilateral loan between a single bank and a borrower. The appropriate type of loan in any situation will depend on the circumstances that may include:

- the purpose for which the customer requires the money, e.g. to finance working capital requirements, or to finance one or more capital expenditures
- the relative costs to the borrower of each different type of lending arrangement
- how the loan capital will be repaid
- whether the borrower wants a committed facility, and
- possibly, the term/duration for which the funds will be required.

Syndicated Loans and Facilities

The traditional term bank loan is provided by a single bank to a customer. This is a bilateral loan, meaning a loan with just two sides or parties to the agreement.

Three factors have created a need for some companies to look to more than one bank for their loans or facilities.

- Their requirements for larger amounts of borrowed funds. There are not many banks big enough to provide the size of loans or facilities needed by some of the largest companies.
- The reluctance of bankers to take on an excessive credit-risk exposure to individual customers. Several banks in recent years have suffered large losses on loans to companies that have gone into liquidation. Not surprisingly, banks have become more rigorous about giving credit, even to large corporate borrowers.
- A greater reluctance by companies to rely on a single bank for funding. Conditions in the lending market vary, but when interest rates are low or falling, there might be a large demand for loans from companies and a large number of banks willing to lend to them. In such circumstances, companies are able to shop around for better interest rates. As a consequence, companies often will be prepared to borrow from a large number of different banks, provided the interest rates are attractive.

As a result of these developments, most companies borrowing in large amounts now use a number of different banks. Borrowing can take the form of:

- syndicated loans
- a number of bilateral loans with several different banks
- a bilateral loan with one bank that the bank then syndicates or sells to other banks by means of transfer (novation), assignment or sub-participation.

Example
A large multinational company wishes to arrange a five-year committed facility of $450 million. It could either:

- find a lead bank willing to arrange a syndication of the facility, or
- try to arrange a number of bilateral loans, for example 15 loans of $30 million each.

Bilateral Loans (perhaps with sub-participation)

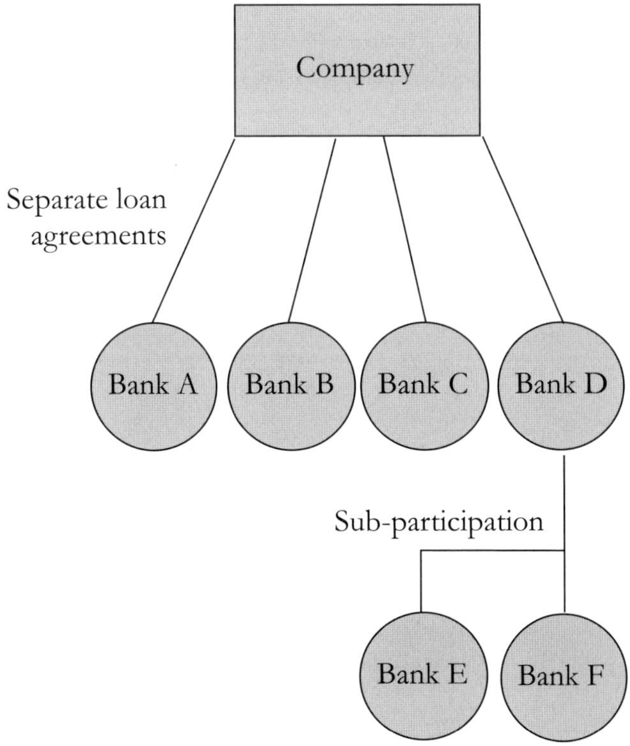

Syndicated Loans

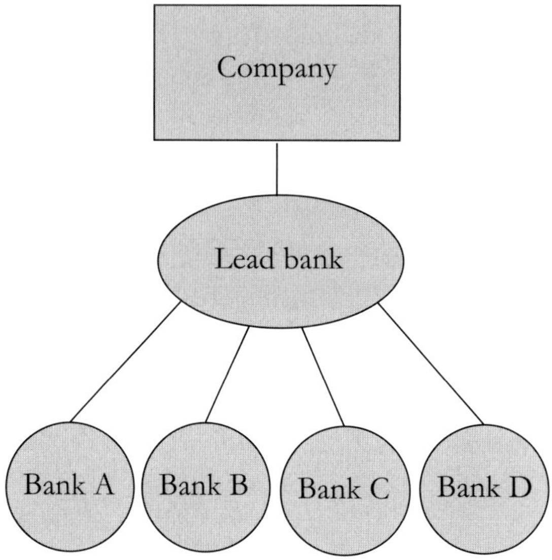

Syndicated Loans

A *syndicated loan* is a term loan to a single borrower from a group (syndicate) of banks. Each bank lends a part of the total amount. Similarly, a *syndicated facility* is a committed revolving-credit facility to a single borrower from a syndicate of banks. Each bank in the syndicate undertakes to make a part of the total facility available for borrowing.

The banks in the syndicate are not affiliated to each other, but are different banks coming together for the purpose of making loan funds available to a borrower.

A syndicated loan or facility may be negotiated when a single bank on its own is unwilling or unable to lend the full amount that a company wants to borrow. The size of the loan or facility is so large that banks consider it more appropriate to share the lending between them.

The main difference between a syndicated loan and a series of bilateral loans with a number of different banks is as follows:

- A syndicated loan is arranged through a single bank, the arranging bank for the syndicate, whereas bilateral loans are negotiated separately with each bank.
- As a consequence, there is just one set of loan documentation to negotiate and agree for a syndicated loan. The loan documentation for bilateral loans has to be negotiated and prepared for each loan separately.

Syndicated loans are an alternative to the bond markets for large amounts of debt funding. Syndicated loan finance can be arranged very quickly and confidentially, and loans can be used to finance major acquisitions. As an example, in its takeover of German group Mannesmann in 1999, UK telecoms company Vodafone arranged a record-breaking facility of €30 billion from a group of 11 banks. Some of this was later re-financed in the bond markets.

The European syndicated loans market, in becoming involved much more in acquisition finance, is developing some of the features of the more mature US loans market. The US loans market is more commoditized, and most loans are given credit ratings by credit agencies, pricing is more market-led and the trading in the secondary loans market is more active.

Arranging a Syndicate

A syndicate of banks is built up. It does not pre-exist. A large company will approach a bank to discuss its borrowing requirements. This bank may consider the amount required to be too much for a bilateral loan, and may suggest a syndicated loan. The first bank to become involved is called the arranger or the arranging bank.

Alternatively, a company might know that its borrowing requirements are sufficiently large to make a syndicated loan arrangement necessary. It might ask several banks to quote a fee rate for the role of arranging bank, and select the keenest quote. Alternatively, the borrower might approach a bank with which it has a good business relationship, and therefore trusts.

The arranger, in agreeing to act for the borrower, will either:

- agree to underwrite the loan at a maximum rate of interest, so that if other banks are unwilling to join the syndicate or lend as much as the borrower requires, the arranger will lend the rest of the money, at no more than the maximum rate it has quoted, or
- promise to use its best endeavors to arrange a syndicate at the lowest interest rates (the finest terms) available. When an arranger acts on a best-endeavors basis, it does not underwrite the loan. It undertakes to do the best it can to find a syndicate of banks willing to lend the money. There is no promise of a maximum interest rate, and the borrower can refuse the interest rates quoted by the syndicate of banks.

It is more usual for the arranger to underwrite the loan, rather than act on a best-endeavors basis.

Arranger

The functions of the arranging bank (or banks) are:

- The arranger will agree the terms of the loan or facility with the borrower.
- It also will underwrite the loan, so that if no other banks agree to join the syndicate, the arranger, as underwriter, will be required to provide all the funds.
- In the case of a large loan or facility, it will find other banks willing to share the underwriting of the loan or facility. These may be called underwriting banks, or lead managers or coarrangers. The lead managers between them will provide the loan funds if they cannot find other banks willing to join the syndicate.
- The lead managers may sub-underwrite a part of the loan that they have underwritten to other banks. The sub-underwriting banks may be called managers in the syndicate.
- The managers may find other banks willing to join the syndicate (participants).

A hierarchy of banks grows up, each bank in the hierarchy committing itself to lending some funds to the borrower, and delegating some, but not all, of its commitment to other banks. A large syndicate is built up not solely by the arranger, but by the arranger together with other banks in the sub-underwriting hierarchy.

The names given to banks in the syndicate hierarchy vary, and terminology is not standard. There may, for example, be an arranger, three or four senior lead managers, six or seven lead managers, a dozen managers and a number of participating banks. Every bank in the hierarchy usually will agree to lend some funds to the borrower.

The borrower usually will require the arranger to provide a large proportion of the loan funds partly because it is important that the arranger should have a direct interest in the lending, and partly because the arranger invariably is a bank with which the borrower has a good relationship. The borrower is likely to be disappointed if the arranger did not lend some of the money.

Being a member of a syndicate is often regarded as a matter of some status and prestige. The borrower will be a well-established organization, and the reason for the syndicated loan might be a prominent news item. The arranger often will have little difficulty in assembling a syndicate for the loan.

Administrative Agent

It is common for just one bank to deal with the routine administration for a syndicated loan. This bank may be known as the agent or the administrative agent. The purpose of having an agent is to simplify the administrative relationship between the borrower and the syndicate, and to avoid the probable confusion that would occur if the borrower had to deal separately with all the banks in the syndicate individually.

The functions of an administrative agent will include:

- Acting as the point of contact with the syndicate for the borrower, and representing the views of the syndicate to the borrower.

- Acting as the point of communication for formal messages between the syndicate and the borrower, for example notifying the borrower of the amount of interest payable for a particular period.
- Monitoring the borrower's compliance with the terms of the loan, for example with warranties and covenants.
- Providing the channel for the flow of funds between the syndicate and the borrower. The agent will be the bank through which the borrower draws down the loan funds, and through which the borrower pays interest and repays capital.

The role of the administrative agent is to make the syndication arrangement work smoothly. The agent does not have the authority to deal with major non-administrative decisions, such as what to do in the event of default by the borrower. Major decisions will be taken either by all the syndicate banks or by a steering committee to which decision-making authority has been delegated.

Steering Committee

Making decisions can present problems for a syndicate, particularly for a large syndicate or a syndicate in which banks assign their loan rights or arrange sub-participation in the syndicate by other banks, so that the banks in the syndicate are continually changing.

Occasionally, important decisions might have to be taken such as when a borrower breaches a loan covenant. Each bank in the syndicate may reserve the right to make its own decision, but an alternative arrangement is for the syndicate to appoint some of their number to a steering committee. Typically, the steering committee will consist of the largest lenders in the syndicate. The syndicate banks will delegate specified decision-making powers to the steering committee.

Arrangements in a Syndicated Loan Agreement

There should be an agreement on how a company should borrow funds within a standby credit facility or revolving credit facility. Broadly, there are two types of arrangement.

In an old-fashioned facility, that is still quite common, a company might borrow from a small syndicate of banks, and draw down the facility from each bank pro rata to its total commitment. For example, suppose that a company has a $80-million facility from a syndicate of five banks whose individual commitments are:

	$m
Bank A	12.0
Bank B	24.0
Bank C	22.0
Bank D	14.0
Bank E	8.0
	80.0

If the company draws down $40 million of the facility (50% of the total) it would borrow from each bank in the syndicate as follows:

		$m
Bank A	(50%)	6.0
Bank B	(50%)	12.0
Bank C	(50%)	11.0
Bank D	(50%)	7.0
Bank E	(50%)	4.0
		40.0

Another arrangement is for each bank in the syndicate to agree to lend up to a specified maximum, but for the borrower to decide within those limits which banks to borrow from, and how much from each, when it wants to draw down funds. The borrower has the opportunity, under this arrangement, to get the banks to compete amongst themselves for the lending business. In this way the borrower might be able to obtain better interest rates

In the previous example, a company drawing down $40 million of an $80 million facility might borrow as follows:

	Amount under-written $m	Amount lent $m
Bank A	12.0	0.0
Bank B	24.0	24.0
Bank C	22.0	2.0
Bank D	14.0	14.0
Bank E	8.0	0.0
	80.0	40.0

Multiple-Option Facility (MOF)

Syndicated bank facilities can have different structures. One such structure is a multiple-option facility or MOF. This is a facility for large corporate borrowers, typically for a term of five to ten years.

A MOF is a form of revolving credit facility, provided by a syndicate of banks. The term multiple option refers to the flexibility within the facility for the borrower to choose in what form to borrow the funds.

- There may be choice in the currencies in which to borrow. The permitted currencies will be specified in the facility agreement.
- More importantly, there will be a choice of debt instruments that can be used within the facility. The borrower will be allowed to borrow for short periods of just a few weeks or a few months (money market loans) or for longer periods from one year to five years. Also, there may be the option of a

Banker's Acceptance facility whereby the borrower can draw bills on a bank in the syndicate. Alternatively, there might be a commercial paper issue whereby the borrower can issue commercial paper and sell it to banks in the syndicate.

An MOF is structured in a similar way to a syndicate for a straightforward syndicated loan. There will be an arranger who initially will underwrite the entire facility. It will appoint other underwriting banks to sub-underwrite a part of the facility: these may be called lead managers or managers for the facility.

The underwriting banks will undertake to provide plain-vanilla loans to the borrower in the event that other participating banks cannot be found for the facility. Plain-vanilla loans are straightforward term loans. These loans would be made available, if required, in the form of a revolving credit facility, and the funds may be referred to as the backstop facility, committed facility or standby facility.

The arranger and other underwriting banks will find banks that are prepared to join a syndicate or tender panel of banks. When the company wants to borrow funds, it decides, possibly in consultation with the arranger, in what form the funds should be raised, for example as a three-month loan, a six-month loan, a two-year loan, a Banker's Acceptance facility or an issue of commercial paper. The banks on the tender panel are invited to tender for the business, and the company can select the bank or banks offering the best rates. The company should be able to obtain keen prices for its borrowings. Banks on the tender panel do not have to offer to lend money, but if they do, they can quote rates of their own choice, i.e. rates at which they would be prepared to lend commercially to the company.

The arranger and the other underwriting banks usually will be on the tender panel of banks. An underwriting bank that is not on the tender panel undertakes to act as a lender of last resort, prepared to lend in the event that the company cannot obtain the funds it requires from the tender-panel banks.

The advantages of an MOF to a company are:

- Its size. It is a facility that might be too large to arrange bilaterally with a single lending bank.
- Its flexibility. The company borrows only the funds that it needs, and for as long as it needs them. It also has flexibility in the choice of method for raising funds, e.g. loans, Banker's Acceptances, etc.
- The MOF is a committed facility. The underwriting banks undertake to provide loans up to the limit of the facility, in the event that the tender panel banks are unwilling to do so.
- Because tender-panel banks are invited to compete to lend funds to the company, the company should be able to borrow at very competitive rates.
- The company can borrow short term or long term within facility and so should be able to choose the most favorable method of raising funds at the time. For example, it may be able to benefit from low short-term interest rates by borrowing short term and then borrowing short term again when the old loan reaches maturity.

MOFs were used quite extensively in the 1980s, but fell out of favor in the 1990s. They are uncommon.

Syndicated Facilities and Covenants

A major drawback to a multi-bank syndicated facility is the potential consequence of a deterioration in the company's financial health to a state where an event of default occurs, or is likely to occur in the near future, and the company's funding has to be renegotiated. A syndicated-facility borrower agrees to the same covenants for all the banks in the tender panel. This can give rise to difficulties in the event of default and the borrower needs either refinancing or a rescheduling of loan payments.

Banks in the syndicate that are not owed money by the customer could refuse any lending on the grounds of the breach of covenant. Banks in the syndicate that have loans outstanding are in much the same position as any lending bank when the customer defaults. However, the banks might disagree about whether the customer should be offered a refinancing package, and if so, which of the syndicate banks should provide the extra money.

For example, when a customer breaches a loan covenant, a small bank that has lent a large amount relative to its size could be very keen on refinancing for the customer in order to protect its loan. On the other hand, a larger bank that is owed very little, might disagree and argue that no further financial support should be given. Obtaining an agreement from all the banks on the tender panel can be very difficult, and could take a long time. If the company's problem is a short-term liquidity shortage rather than a long-term issue of profitability and solvency, any delay by the banks in agreeing to a refinancing package could have disastrous consequences.

Any one bank, out of a total that could be as high as 100 or more, can hold out for terms that are neither acceptable in which case the company could go into liquidation, nor, if accepted, would apply automatically to all other syndicate members.

From the banks' viewpoint a requirement for unanimity gives each bank a reassurance that decisions will not be taken that adversely affect its interests. A bank should not agree to be bound by a majority decision of the banks in the syndicate unless it feels able to depend on them to reach decisions that are in the best interest of all the banks.

If a company is funded by a number of bilateral facilities, discreet negotiations with each bank can be conducted in a refinancing crisis without any single bank having the power of veto.

Transfers, Assignments and Sub-Participation

A lender might not want to wait until the end of the loan period to recover the money lent. The borrower does not have to repay the debt until the redemption date. A lender can recover the money lent, perhaps with some profit or loss on the transaction, by transferring it or selling it to someone else.

A loan is a contractual agreement between the lender and the borrower. The lender undertakes to provide the loan finance. In return the borrower undertakes to pay interest and repay the loan capital. When a lender transfers a debt to someone else, he/she is transferring the right to receive interest from the borrower. These rights have a money value, and the bank making the transfer can sell the loan. The market for selling loans is known as the secondary loan market.

It might seem strange that a bank, having agreed to grant a loan to a borrower, might want to transfer the loan to someone else, but there are several reasons why this might occur.

- The bank might want to change the portfolio of loans in its loan book. For example, a bank might decide that an excessive proportion of its loans have been made to companies in the telecoms sector. It might want to reduce its loans to telecoms companies and lend more to retailing companies. To do this, it can sell or transfer some of its loans to telecoms companies and use the money from the sale to lend to retailing companies.
- A bank might be required to reduce the size of its loan book, i.e. reduce the total amount of loans it makes, for regulatory reasons. Capital adequacy rules are explained in Chapter 9. Briefly, a company must have a minimum amount of capital to support a given volume and quality of business. If a bank's capital is nearing the minimum acceptable level, it will have to increase its capital or reduce its activities, probably by reducing the volume of its loans. It can do this by transferring or selling loans on to another bank or investor.
- A bank might decide that some individual loans are too difficult to manage. A corporate borrower might get into financial difficulties and struggle to meet its loan payment commitments.

A bank might decide to sell the debt to another bank that specializes in handling distressed debt.

When a bank transfers its loan rights to a third party, it might not want the borrower to know about the transfer. If the bank has a long-established commercial relationship with the borrower, or is trying to develop a better commercial relationship, it might prefer to keep quiet about the fact that it is off-loading the customer's debt on to someone else for the sake of good customer relations.

Methods of Transfer

There are three ways for a lender to transfer a loan:

- novation
- assignment
- sub-participation.

Novation

When a bank transfers the loan, it might transfer the rights under the loan agreement, and also certain obligations. *Rights* under a contract can be transferred from seller to buyer by assignment. *Rights and obligations* under contracts can be transferred by novation.

Novation involves:

- canceling the original contract between the old lender and the borrower, and
- creating a new contract between the new lender and the borrower on the same terms and conditions as the old contract.

As a result of novation, effectively the contract remains as it was before, except that the new lender has become a party to the loan agreement in the place of the old lender. Novation can be arranged only with the consent of all three parties, the old lender, the new lender and the borrower.

Novation leaves the old lender with no remaining obligations or rights under the old loan agreement that ceases to exist and is replaced by the new loan.

- Novation transfers the rights and obligations. A lender may retain some obligations under the agreement that the borrower has not yet called on. For example, the borrower might not have drawn all the loan funding available under a revolving credit facility from the lender. A novation arrangement means that the old lender's obligations to provide loan funds up to the limit of the facility can be transferred to the new lender.
- Novation is a method of transferring part of a loan under loan-syndication arrangements. Syndicated loans are explained in Chapter 5.

There can be some difficulties with novation including:

- The consent of all three parties is needed, including the borrower. Unless the borrower agrees to the arrangement, novation is not possible. The borrower might try to strike a hard bargain and negotiate better terms for the new loan agreement.
- The borrower will know about the loan transfer. If the old lender wanted to keep the borrower ignorant of the transfer, novation would be unsuitable.

Assignment

A party to a loan can assign the loan *rights* to another person. Assignment is the sale of those rights to the other person. A party to a contract can only assign rights, *not obligations.*

A lender can assign his rights to be paid by a borrower, but he/she cannot assign any remaining obligations under the loan agreement, for example to provide further loans under a committed loan-facility arrangement.

The advantages of legal assignment are:

- although *the borrower must be notified in writing*, the borrower's consent is not required
- on being notified of assignment, the borrower is required to make the remaining loan payments to the assignee
- if the assigned loan is secured, the assignor's rights usually will be assigned with the debt.

Sub-participation

Sub-participation is another arrangement for transferring all or part of a loan that leaves the original loan agreement unchanged in all respects.

The lending bank takes a deposit from another bank, the sub-participant, equal to all or part of the original loan. The terms of the deposit match the terms of the original loan, or part of it.

For example, suppose that a bank has lent $10 million to a company that is repayable in four years' time. Interest is payable six-monthly at LIBOR plus 1%, on set dates up to the redemption date. The bank might decide to transfer the loan by sub-participation. The sub-participant bank will pay a deposit to the lending bank. The deposit will be for the whole amount of the loan ($10 million) or just part of it. The term of the deposit will match the remaining term of the loan. Interest payments on the deposit also will reflect the interest payments on the loan, i.e. at LIBOR plus 1% on set dates.

In effect, the lending bank has transferred the loan to the sub-participant.

A significant condition of a sub-participation agreement is that the sub-participant receives only payments on the deposit when the lending bank receives payments on the loan from the borrower. If the borrower fails to make a loan payment to the lender, the lender is not required to make any payment to the sub-participant. The sub-participant takes on the credit risk for the loan.

The original lender has obligations to the sub-participant, but these are matched by the rights under the original loan. The obligations are conditional on the borrower meeting his/her obligations under the original loan.

- Sub-participation does not involve the transfer of any rights or obligations under the original loan. These remain unchanged, and the borrower's obligations are to the original lender. The sub-participation agreement creates new obligations for the original lender in return for the deposit, but these are conditional on the borrower meeting his/her obligations under the original loan agreement.
- The sub-participation agreement is a separate contract between the original lender and the sub-participant bank. If the borrower defaults on his/her loan repayment obligations, the original lender can take action to recover the amounts due. The sub-participant does not have any such right of action against the borrower.

Sub-participation is an example of a non-recourse finance agreement.

An advantage of sub-participation is that there is no requirement to notify the borrower. The existing loan arrangement remains in place, and the borrower makes the loan payments to the original lender. The commercial relationship between the borrower and the lending bank is unaffected because the borrower is unaware of the sub-participation.

The Secondary Loan Market

The transfer of loans by novation, assignment or sub-participation, can be described as a loan sale. The lending bank transfers loan rights, and perhaps obligations, and in return receives a payment from the bank to which the loan rights have been transferred.

Problems with loan transfers can be:

- finding another bank that is willing to pay for the rights
- agreeing the terms and conditions for the loan transfer
- preparing the documentation for the loan transfer
- in some cases, particularly when the transfer involves distressed debt, agreeing a price for the transfer/sale.

Distressed debt is corporate debt where the borrower is in financial difficulties. The lender believes the borrower will, or at least probably will, meet its debt payment obligations, but there will be a continuing risk of late payments or even non-payment. The lender may wish to remove distressed debt from its loan book by selling it, but will have to accept a price below the face value of the loan, i.e. less than the amount of the outstanding loan obligation.

The buyer of distressed debt faces a high risk of default by the borrower. However, since the debt is bought below its face value, the buyer will earn high returns if the borrower does not default.

In December 1996, a group of European lending banks formed the Loan Market Association. The purpose of the association is to promote the development of the secondary market for loans, including the secondary market for syndicated loans and for distressed debt. The Loan Market Association has established a code of practise for the secondary market in loans, and developed both standard settlement procedures for loan-transfer arrangements and also standardized loan-transfer documentation. Standardization has increased the quality of disclosure and injected some liquidity into the secondary loan market in Europe. In addition, all the main credit rating agencies have begun to give ratings to European loans. The value of a credit rating is to help banks judge a fair market value for a loan. For example, a $1,000,000 loan at 6% interest with a high credit rating will be worth more than a $1,000,000 loan at 6% but with a low credit rating. Being able to judge fair value helps to stimulate the secondary loans market.

Summary

Small companies obtain bank finance through bilateral loans, facilities and credit lines. Many companies have large borrowing requirements that individual banks are unwilling or unable to meet in full, mainly because of the high credit risk.

Large borrowers must obtain bank finance by means of several bilateral loans, or through a syndicated loan or facility.

Borrowers wishing to decide whether to seek bilateral loans or syndicated facilities could find that their choice is restricted by conditions in the lending market.

However, bilateral arrangements with more than 15-25 banks could become administratively cumbersome. As bilateral loans have become more acceptable to banks, there has been a tendency for large companies and large banks to gravitate towards each other, and for secondary loans sales to become more widespread.

6

Secured or Unsecured Borrowing

Even though lenders and creditors expect the borrower or debtor to pay what they owe under the terms of their agreement, there is always a risk of default. In the case of a borrower, there is always some risk that the borrower will fail to make the interest payments, or will be unable to repay the principal at the end of the term of the loan. The purpose of obtaining security is to protect the lender or creditor against this risk.

If a debt is secured, the security gives the lender or creditor a right, ahead of other lenders or creditors, to look for payment from the secured assets.

Securing a loan is a form of safety net, or second line of defence. It is not something that a lender should want to use, but it takes some of the risk out of lending. It puts the lender in a better position than if the debt were not secured.

- A bank might be prepared to lend to a customer with security when it would not be willing to lend to the same customer with no security.
- The interest rate on a secured loan is likely to be lower than that on an unsecured loan to the same customer.

Security gives a lender a claim over certain assets that are normally assets of the borrower, to support payment of the loan.

Why take security?

The main reasons why taking security improves the likelihood of payment are:

- in the event that the borrower becomes unable to pay its debts, the secured lender or creditor has priority for payment out of the proceeds of the secured assets, over most unsecured creditors and over lower-ranked secured creditors
- the secured lender or creditor is able to *take action* to enforce the security, for example by taking possession of the secured assets, selling them and using the proceeds to repay the loan
- in the case of a secured charge or mortgage, the realizable value of the secured asset or assets normally will be sufficient to repay the secured loan in full.

When a borrower is required to give security for a loan, the threat of what action the bank might take in the event of default often will help to focus the mind of the borrower on the need to meet the payment obligations under the loan agreement. Security can act as a discipline on the borrower. This is particularly the case when an owner-director of a private company is required to give a personal guarantee for a loan from the bank to his company.

Although a bank often will take security for a loan, some lending is unsecured.

- A bank might decide that the credit risk is not significant enough to justify taking security. However, the interest rate charged on an unsecured loan is likely to be higher than interest on a secured loan to the same borrower.
- The borrower might have a good reason for not giving security. For example, it might be prevented from giving security under a negative pledge clause in a different loan agreement. (See Chapter 7.)
- A bank might agree to provide an unsecured loan to win business from a prestigious and potentially valuable customer, for example a major multinational company.

Types of Security

Security might be obtained in a variety of ways. The type of security provided in any situation will depend largely on the nature of the assets that are offered as security.

Security can operate in one of two ways.

- The lender or creditor might take physical possession of the assets that provide the security, and will not surrender the assets to the borrower or debtor until the debt has been paid. Examples of this type of security are a **pledge** and a **lien**.
- The borrower or debtor might keep physical possession of the assets that provide the security, and will continue to use the assets. However, the lender or creditor has some rights over the assets that can be exercised in the event that the loan or debt is not paid. **Mortgages** and **charges** are examples of this type of security.

Most secured loans are of the proprietary type, such as a charge or mortgage, whereby the borrower has the use of the secured assets but the lender retains some rights over them in the event of default.

Pledge

A pledge provides security by giving the lender (creditor) either physical or constructive possession of an asset of the borrower (debtor). The lender retains the asset until the loan is repaid, and has an implied right to sell the asset to recover the debt if the borrower defaults.

Perhaps the most well-known example of pledging assets is giving an item of value to a pawnbroker as security for a loan. If a loan isn't repaid, the pawnbroker has the right to sell the pledged asset and use the proceeds from the sale to recover the debt. If the loan is repaid, the pawnbroker returns the asset to the borrower and the asset is no longer pledged.

A pledge is not a common form of security for a bank loan because there are limited circumstances in which possession of assets, either physical or constructive, can be given to a bank.

Documents may be pledged as security for a loan, but only if possession of the document gives its holder the title to the underlying asset or benefit.

- Documents that might be pledged include bearer securities and, in connection with foreign trade, bills of lading. A bill of lading is a transportation document that gives its holder title to the goods being transported.
- Documents that cannot be used as a pledge include certificates for registered securities. This is because the certificate is merely evidence of title but does not confer title on its holder.

Lien

A lien is the right of a creditor to retain physical possession of a debtor's property until the debt is paid. A lien is similar to a pledge, in the sense that the lender or creditor takes physical possession of the debtor's assets as security. However, a lien differs from a pledge in several ways:

- The borrower agrees to assets being taken as a pledge. The borrower's agreement is not required for a lien.
- A creditor has an implied right to sell pledged assets to recover the debt. In most circumstances, a creditor does not have the right to sell assets held under a lien. If the debtor fails to pay the debt, the lender can continue to hold the assets, but would have to seek payment through the courts. For example, if an automobile owner refuses to pay for repairs done to his/her automobile, the garage that carried out the repairs can hold on to the vehicle until the debt is paid. A common-law lien does not give the creditor the right to sell the asset to recover the debt.

Charge

A charge is a form of security that transfers to the lender (chargeholder) neither the possession nor the ownership of the assets provided as security unless and until the lender enforces the security. The borrower retains the ownership and possession of the assets and the use of them. However, when an enforcement event or crystallization event occurs, the lender has the right to enforce the security and appoint a receiver to sell the charged assets and use the proceeds to repay the debt.

There are two types of charge, a fixed charge and a floating charge.

Fixed Charge

A fixed charge is a charge over one or more specific assets of the borrower as security for a debt. The borrower retains ownership and possession of the charged asset, and can use the asset but cannot dispose of the asset without the lender's (chargeholder's) permission.

A fixed charge gives the chargeholder the right to enforce the security if an enforcement event occurs. Circumstances in which an enforcement event will occur are specified in the document creating the charge and will include failure by the borrower to meet the loan-payment obligations. When an enforcement event occurs, the borrower is in default and the lender can take possession of the charged assets and sell them or, more likely, appoint a receiver to sell the assets. The fixed charge gives the lender prior rights to the proceeds from the sale over the claims of other creditors of the borrower.

- If the sale proceeds exceed the amount of the debt, the debt is repaid in full and the remaining money is available to the borrower, or in the event of a winding up of the borrower, to other creditors.
- If the sale proceeds are less than the amount of the debt, they are used to repay as much of the loan as possible, leaving the lender as an unsecured creditor for the unpaid balance.

Floating Charge

A fixed charge can be created only over assets that a borrower expects to keep in its possession for the duration of the term of the loan, or the borrower could dispose of with the lender's permission.

A floating charge is a form of charge that allows the borrower to dispose of assets that are subject to the charge:

- without the need for the lender's consent, and
- giving the purchaser of any such assets good title to them.

However, when the borrower acquires replacement assets that fall within a class of assets subject to the floating charge, they become subject to the floating charge automatically. A floating charge allows the borrower to trade its assets unencumbered but the charge applies to all current and future assets of the borrower in the charged group of assets.

A floating charge is suited to a company's assets that are continually turned over in the normal course of trade, such as trade debtors and stock in trade, including raw materials and components, finished goods, goods for resale, etc. These often consist of a large number of small individual items, and a floating charge will cover all the assets of a particular type or class, such as all the borrower's stock in trade, or all the borrower's trade debtors.

A floating charge also is applied more widely, to all the business and assets or the undertaking and assets of the borrower. This type of floating charge creates a charge over all the assets used by the borrower in its business, but allows the borrower to dispose of any of those assets without encumbrance.

A lender may take a fixed charge over some specific assets of the borrower and a floating charge over the borrower's undertaking and assets.

The nature of a floating charge

A floating charge is provided as security for a group of assets that may change over time, increasing in value and amount up and down in the course of the borrower's business. In contrast to a fixed charge that is given over specific, defined assets, a floating charge is applied to a group of assets such as the borrower's stock in trade or trade debtors, or to the entire undertaking and assets of the borrower.

Assets acquired by the borrower *after* the floating charge has been created that belong to a category of assets that is subject to the charge, become subject to the charge.

Where assets are subject to a floating charge, the assets are changing continually or from time to time. Stock is used or resold, and replaced by new stock. Existing debtors pay what they owe, but the company continues to sell its goods or services on credit, and new debtors are created. Even fixed assets change from time to time as old plant and machinery, for example office equipment, is replaced.

When a charge over assets is floating, the company is free to deal with the assets, and it does not have to pay the creditor from the proceeds from those assets. For example:

- When there is a floating charge over the trade debts of a company, the company is not required to use the money collected from its debtors to pay the secured lender. The only requirement is that the company eventually should pay the lender on whatever terms have been agreed. This situation will not change unless the lender enforces the charge, and the lender will do this only if the company is in default with the payment of the debt.
- Similarly, a floating charge over the stock in hand of a company means it is free to carry on its business, using the stock or reselling the stock. It is not required to pay the creditor out of the proceeds of any particular stock items, unless and until the creditor enforces the charge.

Crystallization of a floating charge

Assets subject to a floating charge are unencumbered by the charge that hovers over them. However, the lender (chargeholder) can enforce the security when a crystallization event occurs, and the floating charge crystallizes. When a floating charge crystallizes:

- it becomes a fixed charge over all the assets in the class or classes subject to the charge, that the borrower possesses
- the lender (chargeholder) may enforce the charge by appointing a receiver. The power to appoint a receiver usually is included as a term in the document creating the charge; otherwise the chargeholder may apply to the court for a receiver to be appointed.

When, as is often the case, the floating charge covers substantially the whole of the borrower's assets and the charge crystallizes, the chargeholder can appoint an administrative receiver who will realize the secured assets that are subject to the charge, for the benefit of the chargeholder.

Mortgage

A *fixed charge* leaves the borrower as the owner of an asset provided as security, but creates an encumbrance that attaches to the asset. The asset cannot be disposed of without permission of the chargeholder. A *mortgage* is like a fixed charge in various respects, and is given over a specific asset or assets. However, a mortgage transfers ownership of the asset to the lender.

The features of a mortgage are:

- Ownership of the assets is transferred to the lender (mortgagee).
- The mortgagee has the right to sell the asset if the borrower defaults. A bank mortgage over land normally gives the bank the right to take possession of the mortgaged asset at any time, even if the borrower is not in default. However, a bank will not exercise its rights of possession and sale unless the borrower defaults.

- If and when the loan is repaid, the mortgagee is under an obligation to transfer ownership of the assets back to the mortgagor (borrower).

Most types of asset could, in theory, be mortgaged, but usually assets used as security in a mortgage are land and buildings, shares, ships and aircraft.

Standard Security Clauses

Banks use standard security clauses in lending agreements. These can include:

- a continuing security clause
- an all-monies clause
- a repayment-on-demand clause, and
- an indemnity clause.

A *continuing security clause* ensures that the security covers whatever the borrower owes to the bank at any time, and not just the original loan. The security will cover any further lending after the original loan has been granted.

An *all-monies clause* ensures that the security covers all debts of the customer to the bank existing at any time and on any account. This includes any interest due and any expenses incurred by the bank in enforcing its security.

A *repayment-on-demand clause* secures the borrower's agreement to repay on demand what is owed. This clause can be important because the bank's power of sale over charged property is exercisable only when the money becomes due. This can mean waiting to enforce the security even when it is apparent that the borrower is in financial difficulty. The clause allows the bank to demand payment at any time and then sell the charged assets when payment is not forthcoming.

An *indemnity* permits the bank to recover from the borrower all the costs it incurs in taking, keeping and realizing the security. In legal terms, the borrower undertakes to indemnify the bank for these costs.

Quasi-Security

The reason why a lender takes security is to improve the probability that the loan will be repaid. The effect of taking security is to give the lender, in one way or another, some rights over the assets of the borrower. There are other measures that might be taken to protect a lender from losses on a loan or on giving credit that do not involve the lender or creditor in taking rights over the borrower's assets. These types of measure are referred to collectively as quasi-security.

Forms of quasi-security include:

- guarantees
- letters of comfort.

Guarantee

A guarantee is a promise given by one person (a guarantor) to a lender, in which the guarantor undertakes to be answerable for the debt and any default of a borrower. The lender will call on the guarantee, and demand payment from the guarantor, only if it is unable to obtain payment from the borrower.

When a lender calls on a guarantee, the guarantor will be required to pay what the borrower owes up to the amount of borrowing that has been guaranteed. If the bank has called in the loan or advance, the guarantor would be required to pay all the borrower's liabilities, i.e. principal plus unpaid interest, and perhaps also unpaid fees or commissions owed to the bank.

Guarantees often are taken when a bank lends to a company.

- In lending to small private companies, a bank may take a personal guarantee from an owner-director for the bank's lending to the company. This guarantee makes the individual personally liable for the company's debts to the bank, and so prevents the individual from seeking protection behind the limited liability status of the company.
- In lending to a company within a group of companies, a bank often will take a guarantee from another company in the group, typically the parent company. This will prevent the group from winding up the subsidiary that has borrowed the money, leaving the rest of the group unaffected. The provision of a loan to a subsidiary might be made conditional on the parent company giving a satisfactory guarantee.

Continuing guarantees

A guarantee may be single or continuing. A single guarantee applies to just one lending transaction. When a guarantee is required for a borrower's overdraft, or for a revolving credit facility, there are a number of transactions as the borrower draws funds under the lending agreement and also pays money back into the account. The amount of the borrower's debt will fluctuate and in such cases the guarantee should be a **continuing guarantee**, and described as such in the guarantee agreement.

Letter of Comfort

A parent company might refuse to give a guarantee for a loan from a bank to one of its subsidiaries, and have a plausible and acceptable reason for its refusal. For example, it may be prevented from giving a guarantee because it would breach a loan covenant by doing so, or, in the case of a foreign parent company, it may be prevented by its national law. A company might even refuse to give a guarantee on the grounds that it is contrary to the company's policy to give guarantees.

A bank might be willing to forgo a guarantee if it is given a letter of comfort instead. A letter of comfort, also known as a letter of intent, is intended to give some reassurance (comfort) to the bank regarding its loan to the subsidiary.

The contents of a letter of comfort can vary widely.

- It might give an acknowledgement from the parent company that it is aware of the existence of the loan to the subsidiary, and of the subsidiary's debt obligations to the bank.
- It might go further, and not just acknowledge the existence of the loan. It also might state that it is the parent company's intention to maintain its investment in the subsidiary, and that it is its intention or policy to ensure that all its subsidiary companies should be capable of meeting their debt obligations.

A letter of comfort usually is not intended to be a binding undertaking by its provider, and so is a document of doubtful value to a lending bank. A bank relying on such a letter will be putting its trust in the moral rectitude of its provider, or the parent company's reputation.

Lender's Rights in a Liquidation

Bank loans and other debt instruments can be grouped into three categories:

- Senior debt
- Junior debt
- Subordinated loans.

Senior debt consists of secured loans that rank ahead of other creditors, to the extent that the loan is covered by the value of the security, in the event of liquidation of the company.

Junior debt is unsecured loan stock that ranks with other unsecured creditors in a liquidation.

A subordinated loan is an unsecured loan that usually ranks behind other unsecured creditors in a liquidation.

The Value of Security

Security on a loan is not always what it seems. Banks have lent extensively in the past on the traditional security of a mortgage on property, but have still lost huge sums of money when the borrower defaulted on repayments. The sell-off value of the secured assets was much less than the amount outstanding on the loan. When banks consider lending against the security of property, they look at lending values. The lending value of a property is the percentage of its supposed market valuation. For example, if the lending value is 75%, a bank will lend 75% of the property's market value, secured against the property perhaps by a mortgage. Lending values usually are set for bank managers by a head-office decree, known as formula lending. The margin between 100% and the lending value represents the buffer between the bank and loss on default. A fall in property values can erode this buffer and expose the bank to the risk of loss.

Example

Omega Bank lent $20 million to Alpha Corporation with a bullet repayment schedule. The three-year loan was secured against property valued at $25 million. A year or so later, Alpha went into liquidation, leaving the loan unpaid. The market value of the secured property was $17.5 million at most and possibly as little as $15 million in an enforced sale.

Analysis

Omega Bank will take possession of the property. By selling it immediately, it would record a loss of between $2.5 million and $5 million, depending on the sale price. Alternatively, it could hold on to the property and hope for a rise in market prices before trying to sell it.

Covenants, Warranties and Events of Default

Normally a bank will provide term loans, secured as well as unsecured, or committed facilities only on condition that the customer agrees to certain loan covenants. Covenants, other than a cross-default covenant, usually are not built into overdraft agreements.

A *covenant* is a written undertaking by a borrower to comply with a specified condition of lending. Each loan agreement will contain a number of covenants. They must be negotiated carefully and constructively between the bank and the borrower. The borrower should try not to concede too much. The bank should insist on covenants that protect its position. The loan price, bank fees and interest rate charged, will be influenced by the degree of comfort that the bank obtains from the covenants in the loan agreement.

A borrower also will be required to give certain *representations* to the lender. Representations that are written into the loan agreement become either *warranties* or loan *conditions*.

Types of Covenant

Covenants fall into two broad categories:

- positive covenants, and
- restrictive or negative covenants.

Covenants can be qualitative or quantitative.

- A qualitative covenant is an undertaking of a non-quantifiable

nature, designed to protect the lender against loss.
- A quantitative covenant is a measurable benchmark standard of performance, typically financial performance, or a financial constraint to which the borrower agrees to be bound.

Positive covenants are qualitative. Restrictive covenants can be qualitative or quantitative. A typical loan agreement might include three or four quantitative covenants.

Positive Covenants

Positive covenants, sometimes referred to as boilerplate covenants, are undertakings by the borrower to take certain actions, often at regular intervals during the term of the loan. Examples of positive covenants are listed below.

Positive covenants

The borrower undertakes to:	provide the bank annually with a copy of its audited financial statements
	provide the bank regularly, usually monthly or quarterly, with financial statements from the company's internal management accounts
	submit certificates at regular intervals signed by a director or the company secretary, that the company is still in compliance with its loan agreement
	maintain its assets in good condition, fully insured
	retain its corporate existence. For example, it must not put itself into voluntary liquidation, or switch from the status of a company to the status of a partnership.

Restrictive Qualitative Covenants

A restrictive or negative covenant is a promise by the borrower not to do something. In a loan agreement with a long list of covenants, most are likely to be restrictive covenants of a qualitative nature. Some of the most significant qualitative covenants are:

- a negative pledge
- a cross-default clause, and
- a material adverse change clause.

Negative Pledge

A negative pledge is an undertaking by the borrower that it will not create a class of creditor that ranks above the lending bank in the hierarchy of creditors. For example, if a loan were unsecured, the borrower would give a covenant not to provide security for any new borrowing it arranges in the future so long as the loan remains unpaid. Similarly, if the loan were secured by a floating charge over the assets and an undertaking of the borrower, a negative pledge would be an undertaking by the borrower not to give a fixed charge or mortgage over any of its property on any new borrowing in the future so long as the loan remains unpaid.

A negative pledge can be a serious restriction for a company with a continuing need to borrow because it can act as a restriction on new secured borrowing.

Example

A company borrows $10 million unsecured from a bank, and gives a negative pledge that it will not create a higher-ranking class of creditors while the loan is still outstanding. The company, having borrowed the $10 million, then wants to raise a further $5 million. Another bank agrees to lend the money, but only if it is secured against fixed assets of the company.

Analysis

The negative pledge on the first loan would prevent the company from agreeing to this condition for the new loan. To overcome the problem, it could ask the original lending bank to waive the covenant. However, a negative pledge, once agreed, is rarely waived by a lending bank. The only other way to overcome the restriction would be to repay the original loan. The company could then try to borrow $15 million, and use $10 million of this funding to repay the initial loan.

Cross-Default Clause

Often banks will look for additional comfort from a covenant requiring that if the borrower is in default on any one of its loans or banking transactions above a certain value, this will create a default automatically on every other loan or banking contract. This type of covenant is called a cross-default clause.

A cross-default clause usually is quantified to some extent, so that a minimum size of default must occur before cross default is triggered. This could be a percentage, perhaps 1% or 2%, of shareholders' funds, or a monetary threshold, such as $1 million to $10 million.

For example, a company that fails to repay a loan of $7.5 million automatically would be in default on all its other loans and guarantees that are subject to a cross-default covenant with a threshold in excess of less than $7.5 million. When cross-default is triggered, a company's financial position is often irrecoverable. Normally there is a period of grace, specified in the covenant, before non-payment of interest or principal becomes an event of default. This is to allow for missed or misdirected payments and other administrative errors.

Example

A company that has existing loans totalling $5 million negotiates a new loan of $7 million. The new loan agreement includes a cross-default clause, whereby a default on a loan of $1 million or more will trigger the cross-default.

Analysis

If the borrower fails to repay the loan principal on a maturing bullet loan of $500,000, the cross-default is not triggered. However, if the borrower then fails to repay a $1 million loan, the cross-default will be triggered, and the borrower will be in breach of its covenant on the $7 million loan as well as in breach of its agreement on the $1 million loan.

Material Adverse Change Clause

Banks often seek a covenant that makes it an event of default if there is a material adverse change in the company's financial, or, in some circumstances, commercial position.

There is no precise legal definition of what constitutes a material adverse change, and a covenant in a loan agreement normally permits the bank to use its judgment in deciding when such a change has occurred. A bank can decide that there has been an event of default, even if the borrower does not think so, and insist on immediate repayment by accelerating the loan.

The borrower can sue the bank if it disagrees, but any court judgment would be delayed by the process of law. By this time, the company could have gone into liquidation for lack of those funds.

Material-adverse-change clauses are applied mainly to syndicated loan arrangements rather than bilateral loans. They originated in the 1970s with syndicated loans to sovereign borrowers. It is difficult to devise workable covenants for loans to governments, and a material-adverse-change clause was set up to provide some comfort to the lending banks.

Other Qualitative Covenants or Warranties

Loan agreements may include a large number of other undertakings by the borrower that are either restrictive qualitative covenants or warranties.

For example, a borrower might undertake that it will *not*

- borrow further until the current loan is repaid
- give third-party guarantees to other banks on behalf of other borrowers

- merge with or take over another company during the term of the loan or facility
- sell material fixed assets of its business unless new assets are purchased to replace them, or unless the proceeds are used to repay all or part of the loan. This is known as an *alienation-of-assets* clause.

Quantitative Covenants

Quantitative covenants are financial undertakings setting limitations on a borrower's financial position so long as the loan remains outstanding. The most common examples of quantitative covenants are:

- a net-worth test
- restrictions on secured borrowing
- an interest-cover test
- a minimum net-worth requirement
- a minimum current ratio requirement.

Net-Worth Test (Gearing-Ratio Covenant)

The net-worth test, also called the debt ratio or gearing-ratio covenant, restricts the total amount of debt that the borrower can incur. The limit is expressed as a gearing ratio.

Financial gearing is measured in various ways, all similar in concept. In general terms, it is the ratio of a company's interest-bearing debts to equity share capital and reserves. A gearing-ratio covenant sets a maximum limit to the company's permitted gearing ratio as defined by the loan agreement.

The borrowing company agrees that its total borrowings, excluding any pre-agreed exceptions, should not exceed a given percentage of the shareholders' funds, i.e. of share capital, plus retained earnings, plus other equity reserves. This limit normally is set at between 100% and 175% of shareholders' funds.

Example

Alpha arranged a five-year $30 million committed facility with Omega Bank. At the time the facility was agreed, Alpha's net worth, measured as the balance sheet value of its shareholders' funds, was $32 million. Alpha already had a term loan of $10 million.

The new loan agreement included a covenant that Alpha's total borrowings should not exceed 120% of the value of its shareholders' funds. At the start of the term of the facility, Alpha drew down $15 million.

Analysis

When Alpha borrowed $15 million, its financial position was as follows:

	$
Old loan	10 million
New borrowings	15 million
Total loans	25 million
Shareholders' funds	32 million

Loans as a percentage of shareholders' funds were 78.125% (25 ÷ 32 x 100%).

Suppose that Alpha subsequently makes a loss of $7 million, and wants to draw down a further $10 million of the committed facility. The bank can refuse because the net worth covenant would be breached.

	$
Current loans	25
New borrowing required	10
Total borrowing required	35
Shareholders' funds ($32 million minus loss of $7 million)	25

Loans as a percentage of shareholders' funds would now be 140% (35 ÷ 25 x 100%).

Alpha could restrict its new borrowings under the facility to $5 million, bringing its total loans to $30 million or 120% of shareholders' funds. However, if Alpha continues to make losses, it will be in breach of the net-worth covenant because of the decline in shareholders' funds caused by the losses.

Restrictions on Secured Borrowing

As a subsidiary covenant to a net-worth test, a borrower could agree to accept a restriction on the amount of borrowings that are secured either by a fixed charge on specific assets of the company or in the form of a floating charge over the assets of the company.

This restriction is expressed as a percentage of shareholders' funds, and is somewhere in the range of 10% to 100%, depending upon the nature of the business. A higher percentage is appropriate for businesses where it is usual to borrow heavily with mortgages secured on property, e.g. for property investment companies. A lower percentage is more appropriate for industrial companies where the realizable value of assets in a liquidation could be much lower than their balance-sheet value.

Interest-Cover Test

An interest-cover test is a covenant in which the borrower undertakes that its profit before interest and tax (PBIT) will be at least a specified multiple of the total interest payable by the company in a given period, normally a single financial year. The ratio of PBIT to interest charges is the interest-cover ratio, and a covenant can specify that this must be at least 2.5 times. This figure can be as high as 3.0 or even 4.0 times if the bank wishes to curb excessive levels of debt.

A borrower's interest-cover ratio is calculated from its audited financial statements – its annual report and accounts – although the loan agreement should give the bank the right to examine the calculations or obtain an opinion from an expert, as protection against creative accounting and the manipulation of its reported profits by the borrower.

The loan agreement should specify in some detail how PBIT and interest charges should be calculated to avoid the possibility of a dispute between the borrower and the bank. For example, it should be clear whether or not interest charges should be net of any interest income earned by the company.

In some loan agreements an interest-cover ratio – sometimes known as an income-gearing test – is the only quantitative covenant sought by the banks because even if more covenants were applied, the interest-cover test is probably the first that would be breached.

A company in a cyclical business with an erratic profit stream could try to resist an interest-cover test as a loan covenant because the covenant is likely to be breached as soon as the down-cycle produces a poor trading year.

Minimum Net Worth

A company can be required to maintain the value of its shareholders' funds at a minimum monetary amount. If shareholders' funds fall below this amount, lenders to the company could be at risk, and a breach of covenant would occur. For example, a company could undertake to maintain the value of its shareholders' funds at not less than $200 million. Dropping below $200 million would represent a breach of covenant. The minimum net worth normally is set slightly lower than the borrower's net worth as at the start of the loan period.

This covenant gives a warning to the lender about losses by the borrower because losses reduce the value of shareholders' funds and consequently represent a threat to the company's lenders. To be effective the minimum value of shareholders' funds should be increased broadly in line with the net worth of the company as it grows. This is because retained profits accumulate and boost the value of shareholders' funds. A minimum net worth agreed several years earlier could cease to have any practical value as a constraint on the company's financial management.

Example

Gamma, whose shareholders' funds are worth $100 million, borrows $80 million from Epsilon Bank for a five-year term. A covenant in the loan agreement is that Gamma's net worth must not fall below $80 million.

Analysis

Gamma will be in breach of the covenant if it incurs losses of more than $20 million, reducing its net worth below $80 million.

Suppose that Gamma is profitable for a time, and retained profits boost its net worth to $125 million. Gamma then borrows another $40 million from another bank, Central Bank.

The minimum net-worth covenant in the loan agreement between Gamma and Epsilon Bank is now of little value. Gamma would have to incur losses of over $45 million before it is in breach of the covenant, but because its total borrowings are now $120 million, Gamma could run into difficulties with its loan repayments much sooner, should it get into financial difficulties.

Epsilon Bank should have insisted that the covenant provided for a periodic increase in the required minimum net worth of Gamma, in line with its changing financial position.

Minimum Current Ratio Clause

The current ratio is the value of a company's current assets expressed as a multiple of its current liabilities.

$$\text{Current ratio} = \frac{\text{Current Assets}}{\text{Current Liabilities}}$$

A covenant can specify that this must not fall below a certain value. A bank can insist on this covenant, particularly for businesses that could have liquidity problems. The minimum ratio required by the bank can vary according to:

- the cash generative nature of the borrower's business
- the length of the production cycle, if the borrower is a manufacturing company
- the speed of stock turnover in the business.

A bank will look for a minimum ratio of between 1.0 and 1.5 to act as an early warning of an impending liquidity crisis.

Typically the threshold level will be higher for a business that manufactures products for stock, e.g. a manufacturer of consumer durable goods, and lower for a business with a fast stock turnover ratio, such as food retailers.

Other Quantitative Covenants

Other quantitative covenants are much less common, but can be included in a loan agreement. Examples are listed below.

- A minimum ratio of operational cash flow to the amount of long-term debt maturing in the next 12-month period.
- A maximum limit on annual capital expenditure.
- A maximum limit on dividends to shareholders and on the purchase of its own shares by the company.
- A minimum amount of working capital, i.e. the value of current assets minus current liabilities.

Covenants and Takeover Bids

A loan agreement could include a covenant preventing the borrower from making a takeover bid for another company during the term of the loan. Where such a covenant does not exist, a takeover bid by an indebted company could put it at risk of breaching its loan agreement. A target company in a takeover bid could use this claim in its defence against the bidder.

Representations and Warranties

Representations are statements made by a borrower to a lending bank before the loan agreement is signed that are intended to have the effect of making the bank agree to provide the loan or facility. When a representation is included in the actual loan-agreement document, it becomes a term of the contract, either a condition or a warranty.

Representations and warranties have three main purposes.

- Representations are used to *extract information* from the borrower. The information received helps the bank to reach its decision about lending to the borrower, and the terms of the lending agreement.
- By including representations in the loan agreement, as conditions or warranties, they give the bank contractual remedies against the borrower in the event that any of the representations were untrue. For example, if a company arranges a revolving credit facility, and a warranty in the lending agreement is found to be untrue, the bank can refuse to allow the borrower to draw down any more funds under the facility arrangement.
- A breach of a warranty also gives a bank the right to legal remedies, including damages.

Representations and warranties are either legal or commercial. Examples of legal reps and warranties would be statements by the borrower that it is properly incorporated under the laws of its jurisdiction, and that it has the capacity under its articles of association to borrow funds. Examples of commercial reps and warranties are statements by the borrower that no insolvency proceedings against it have been started, that there is no actual or impending litigation against it that could result in a harmful and expensive adverse judgment in the courts.

As stated earlier, representations that are written into a loan agreement become terms of the contract, and are either a warranty or a condition of the contract.

- A condition is something vital to the contract, and a breach of condition will be an event of default, giving the lender the right to terminate the loan agreement.
- A warranty is a less important term in the contract, and a breach of warranty usually is not sufficient for the lender to terminate the contract. However, a lender may take legal action

for damages in the event of a breach of warranty by the borrower.

Event of Default

An event of default is something that occurs to put a borrower in breach of a loan agreement. If a default occurs, the lender can declare, if it so wishes, that the loan principal and any accrued unpaid interest must be paid in full immediately. If the borrower does not comply with this demand, the lender can take legal action to recover the amounts due.

The loan documentation will specify what constitutes an event of default. Events of default will include:

- failure to pay interest or loan principal when due
- any breach of a covenant
- breach of a condition
- insolvency of the borrower
- default on another loan where a cross-default clause applies
- a material adverse change in the borrower's business where a material adverse change clause applies.

The action a bank takes when an event of default occurs will depend on the reason for the default. Obviously, if the borrower is insolvent, the bank will take urgent action to protect its position, possibly by taking steps to enforce its security for the loan if it has any. Other defaults, such as a breach of covenant or condition, or even failure to make an interest payment on schedule, should lead to the bank discussing the problem with the borrower and trying to agree a practical, commercial solution, rather than insisting on termination of the loan. It is in a bank's interest to agree a program of measures to remedy the borrower's financial position.

Banks use an event of default as a warning signal that the borrower is in difficulty and that some remedial measures might be necessary.

In a management buyout some years ago, the directors of the company, that was heavily in debt, stated in the buyout document: 'it is not unlikely that an Event of Default will occur in the course of the next three years.... The directors are of the view that the lenders ... are likely to continue to act commercially and realistically and not to demand immediate repayment on non-material or merely technical Events of Default'.

Although a bank is unlikely to demand immediate repayment in an event of default, it may, depending on how serious the breach has been:

- demand a restriction on its future activities by the borrower, and
- ask for a higher interest rate on renegotiating the loan or facility.

Grace Period

A grace period is the time between an event of default and the bank taking action against the borrower to protect its position. A loan agreement will allow a grace period of three to ten days in an event of default due to non-payment of interest, mainly to guard against the possibility of an administrative oversight by the borrower in making the payment, or the possibility of an error in the banking system.

A borrower that expects to breach a loan covenant should discuss the problem with the bank as soon as possible before the breach occurs. Through discussion, an accommodation often can be reached, although the bank will want to monitor the revised loan repayments closely.

Currency of Borrowing

Many companies, particularly companies in multinational groups, now borrow from their banks in foreign currency, for short-term and long-term periods. Currency loans can be obtained by borrowing in the eurocurrency market, or from a domestic bank in the country of the currency's origin.

Eurocurrency Loans

The eurocurrency markets are for borrowing and lending currencies outside their country of origin, usually for terms of up to 12 months and occasionally for longer. In other words, they are short-term currency-loan markets. A UK company, for example, can borrow from a UK bank in dollars, euros, yen or any other freely convertible currency. Similarly, a French company can borrow from a French bank in dollars, sterling, yen and other currencies.

The main eurocurrency market is in eurodollars. Eurodollar loans are priced at a margin above LIBOR and long-term loans are at a floating rate. Fixed-term loans are rare beyond six or 12 months. There are markets for other eurocurrencies, including euros, euroyen, eurosterling, etc..

The markets originated from eurocurrency deposits, money deposited with a bank situated outside the currency's country of origin. A eurodollar, for example, is created when a dollar is transferred from an account with a bank in the US to an account with a bank outside the US. Ownership of the dollars is not relevant to the definition. US dollars deposited with a bank in London are eurodollars, regardless of whether the depositor resides inside or outside the US. Eurodollar deposits are lent to other customers by the non-US bank, creating eurodollar market activity.

Most long-term euroloans are roll-over loans. The bank allows the borrower to roll over the loan for three or six months, at the borrower's choice, at each successive roll-over date.

Some loans also have a multicurrency option, allowing the borrower to switch the currency of borrowing, e.g. from dollars to Australian dollars, on any roll-over date.

Most eurocurrency market lending is between banks. Other financial institutions and large companies also deal direct in the market. However, creditworthy smaller companies wishing to borrow in a foreign currency can do so indirectly, normally at a floating rate of interest, by borrowing from their bank.

Borrowing Abroad

As an alternative to borrowing in the eurocurrency markets through a domestic bank, a company could approach a bank in the currency's country of origin. It could be appropriate for a company to finance the activities of a foreign subsidiary by borrowing in the subsidiary's own country. For example, a UK group wishing to finance operations in the US could try to obtain a dollar loan through its US subsidiary and from a US commercial bank.

Currency Swaps

Companies can manage the currency of their borrowings by means of currency swaps. A currency swap enables a company to borrow long term in one currency, and swap its principal liability and interest-payment obligations into a second currency. For example, a company can borrow in sterling and arrange a swap into dollars. The swap would give the company interest-payment obligations in dollars rather than sterling, and a repayment of principal at the end of the loan term also in dollars.

Currency swaps are now an important feature of the international loans and bond markets.

Intercompany Loans

Multinational groups of companies can arrange their currency-borrowing requirements by using intercompany loans or funds transfers.

Example
Omega Group operates in two countries, the UK and the Netherlands. The group wishes to borrow €20 million to invest in a new project in the Netherlands.

Analysis
The company could raise the money from bank loans in a variety of ways.

- The Dutch subsidiary could borrow the money in its domestic loans market. The UK parent could be required to provide a downstream guarantee.
- The UK parent could borrow euros in the eurocurrency market, and relend the money to its Dutch subsidiary, or transfer the funds by another method, such as purchasing newly issued shares in the subsidiary, denominated in euros. A eurocurrency loan would be fairly short term.
- For long-term borrowing, the UK parent could borrow in sterling and arrange a currency swap into euros.

Bank Lending Strategy

Two factors have a significant influence over the lending policy or strategy of commercial banks:

- bad debts from lending, and
- capital adequacy rules.

The combination of these two problems can lead to a major reassessment by the banks of their lending strategy, particularly when there is a change in economic conditions and the state of the economy.

Bad Debts from Lending

An economic recession can have two serious consequences for lending banks:

- non-repayment of loans by customers, and
- a collapse in property values.

In a recession, many borrowers become unable to meet their loan-repayment obligations because of financial difficulties. There may be a large number of corporate failures, and many other companies may seek to renegotiate their loans and facilities with their banks.

A decline in property values affects the value of the security, where loans are secured against property. In a recession, the value of security may fall at the same time that the risk of default rises.

A continuing problem for lending banks in such circumstances is to decide how many outstanding loans are bad debts that should be written off as losses. Another problem is how to protect the financial position of the banks and improve profitability for the future.

Banks: the Bad Debts Problem and its Consequences

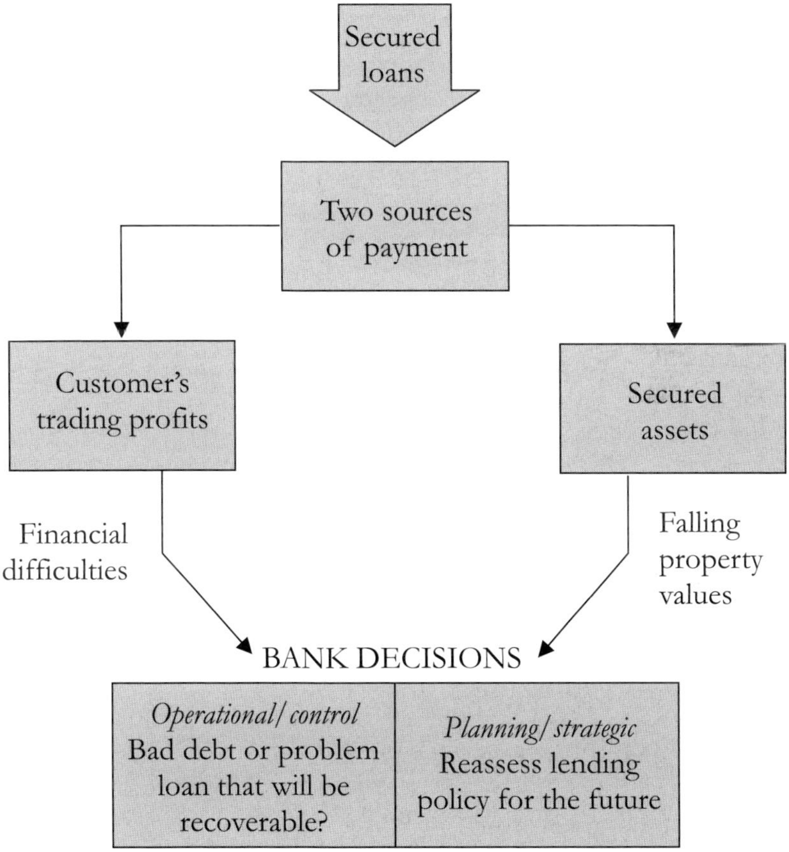

Bad Debts and Lending Margins

It is useful to look at the implications for profits and lending margins in bad debts.

Example

Suppose that the funds of Alpha Bank cost 6% per annum and that the bank can relend these funds at an average margin of 200 basis points (2%) above their cost, i.e. at 8%. One per cent of loans are non-performing and are written off each year as bad debts. No interest on the non-performing loans is credited to income in the bank's profit and loss account. Alpha Bank's loans total $50,000 million.

Analysis

When bad debts are 1% of the loan book, the bank's lending profits are as follows:

	$ million
Margin on loans (2% of 99% of $50,000 million)	990
Bad debts (1% of $50,000 million)	– 500
Profit	490

A sharp increase in bad debts could wipe out the bank's profits. Suppose, for example, that bad-debt provisions in the year totaled 2% of the loan book. The bank would now make a net loss on lending.

	$ million
Margin on loans (2% of 98% of $50,000 million)	980
Bad debts (2% of $50,000 million)	-1,000
Loss	-20

To restore the profit to around $500 million, the bank would have to increase its margin on lending to about 3%, as follows:

	$ million
Margin on loans (3% of 98% of $50,000 million)	1,470
Bad debts (2% of $50,000 million)	-1,000
Profit	470

This example illustrates that when there is an increase in the percentage of non-performing loans, the banks must either suffer a large loss or make up the loss by raising their margins on lending.

Bad Debt Provisions

Banks must decide which of their outstanding customer loans are non-performing, for which the debt probably will never be recovered. These specific bad debt provisions must be distinguished from outstanding loans for which payments are overdue, but which the customer is expected to pay in full after sorting out some short-term financial difficulties. The distinction is important because of the impact on the bank's reported profits.

If a bank believes that an outstanding loan is unlikely to be repaid, it should:

- make a provision for the bad debt in its profit and loss account, and
- exclude the interest on the debt from its income for the year.

If, on the other hand, a bank believes that a customer is a hospital case that can be nursed back to good financial health, and eventually will repay its loan in full with interest, there is no need to make a bad-debt provision in the profit and loss account. Any accrued interest on such loans, although unpaid, can be included as income for the year.

When a provision is made for a bad debt, the amount provided becomes a charge against the profits of the bank.

Example

Interest of $1 million has accrued on a $10 million bank loan. The interest is owing from the customer, but has not yet been paid.

Analysis

If the bank is satisfied that the customer will honor the debt obligations, it will include the interest charge of $1 million in its profit and loss account for the period, and record $10 million as an active loan outstanding and receivable (an asset) in its balance sheet.

If the bank is convinced that the customer will not pay, it could write off the loan. There would be no income from the loan in its profit and loss account, but a loss of $10 million would be reported for the bad debt.

The loan would no longer appear in the balance sheet and the asset will have been written off.

If the bank suspects that the customer will not pay, it can adopt either of two courses of action:

- discuss the problem of interest arrears or non-payment of loan principal with the customer and if necessary agree to a loan refinancing package, or
- create a provision for a doubtful debt.

If the bank arranges a refinancing package to help the customer, it might increase the loan interest charge to $1.2 million. It would report this as income in its profit and loss account, and the $10 million loan as a balance-sheet asset.

However, if the bank remains unhappy about the prospects of repayment, it can create a provision for a doubtful debt. Interest income for the year would be $1 million from the loan, because the loan has not been written off. However, a provision for unpaid interest ($1 million) would be made, together with a provision for a doubtful debt for the loan principal ($10 million). Both new provisions would be charged against the profits of the bank, giving a net loss of $10 million.

	$ million
Loan interest	1
Provision for non-payment of interest	–1
Provision for non-payment of loan	–10
Net loss	–10

In the bank's balance sheet, the new position will be as follows:

	$ million
Loan (asset)	10
Provision for doubtful debt (liability)	10
Net value	0

It is for the bank and its auditors to decide whether to make a bad-debt provision for any loan where payments are overdue. These decisions call for judgment, and banks can take differing views.

Writing off Bad Debts

A provision cannot last forever in a bank's balance sheet. Eventually, the loan must be written off as valueless, and the provision is no longer necessary.

- When a provision is made for a doubtful loan, and the loan subsequently is written off as a bad debt, the loss is recorded when the provision is first created. There is no further loss when the loan is written off.
- When a loan is written off as a bad debt without a provision having been made previously, the loss, equal to the outstanding loan principal and any unpaid accrued interest owing, is recorded when the debt actually is written off.

Specific Provisions and General Provisions

A distinction is made between specific and general provisions for doubtful debts or bad loans. Specific provisions are made when individual loans are identified as non-performing and probably unlikely to be repaid. A general provision is an additional non-specific provision when the bank judges from experience that bad debts will be a certain percentage of total loans, but it cannot yet identify all of them individually.

Capital Adequacy

Capital adequacy, in the case of banks, refers to the need for a bank to have sufficient capital funds of its own as protection for its depositors.

Example

Delta Bank has total assets of $1,000 million. These are financed by customer deposits of $990 million and share capital and reserves of $10 million.

Analysis

If Delta Bank suffered losses on bad loans of $10 million, its share capital and reserves would be wiped out. Customer deposits would be at risk from any further losses because the bank's total assets would be lower in value than its deposit liabilities.

Banking authorities recognize the need to insist on capital adequacy for banks. Conceptually, two ways in which capital adequacy can be measured and controlled are by means of a minimum gearing ratio or by means of a minimum risk-asset ratio. It is useful to look at these concepts because they provide a basis for current banking regulation.

Minimum Gearing Ratio

A bank has two main sources of funds, its own capital and deposits of customers.

A gearing-ratio approach to measuring and controlling capital adequacy is based on the view that the bank's own capital should be not less than a certain proportion of total liabilities. In other words, a bank should have a minimum gearing ratio. For example, if a minimum gearing ratio of 10% is imposed, the ratio of the bank's capital to customer deposits should be not less than 1:9.

Minimum Risk Asset Ratio

A bank's assets consist mainly of loans and investments. Other assets include cash and operational items such as buildings and equipment. The risk of losing money is greater with some assets than with others. Cash is risk-free, but a bank loan could turn into a bad debt.

A risk asset is any asset that could lose value. The risk of loss varies between different types of asset. A weighted risk asset, also called a risk-weighted asset, can be measured as the amount by which the asset could lose value. For example, if a category of assets could lose value by up to 50%, and the total amount of these assets is $100 million, their weighted risk value is $50 million ($100 million x 50%).

Risk assets can be given a weighted risk value by multiplying the amount of each asset by a suitable risk weighting of between 0% and 100%. A risky loan would have a 100% risk weighting, whereas cash (till money) would have zero risk.

Example

Omega Bank has made loans to the government of $50 million, mortgage loans of $80 million, and other loans to companies and individuals of $300 million. Risk weightings are nil for loans to the government, 50% for mortgage loans and 100% for other loans.

The bank also has $20 million of investments in government securities that have a 20% risk weighting.

Analysis

The weighted risk assets of Omega Bank are as follows:

Item	**Assets** **$m**	**Risk weighting** **%**	**Risk-weighted assets** **$m**
Government loans	50	0	0
Mortgage loans	80	50	40
Other loans	300	100	300
Investments	20	20	4
Total	450		344

Capital adequacy could be measured by a risk-asset ratio. This is a ratio of the bank's capital to its weighted risk assets. A bank could be required to maintain a minimum ratio of capital to weighted-risk assets.

To establish capital adequacy requirements using a risk-asset ratio approach, there must be precise definitions of:

- what constitutes capital, and specifications for how much capital and what type of capital a bank should possess, and

- what constitutes risk assets, and how they should be weighted in value. For example, should off-balance sheet transactions, such as standby facilities, documentary credits, financial guarantees, or foreign-exchange positions, be included as risk assets?

The Basle Agreement

Banking regulators have long recognized the need for capital adequacy. However, until the Basle Agreement of 1987 was adopted by the banking regulators of the major economies of the world, the authorities in each country applied their own rules to decide whether banks met acceptable standards of capital adequacy and liquidity.

Differing national regulations resulted in complaints by some international banks that rival banks from other countries had a competitive advantage because easier rules on capital adequacy in their country allowed them to lend more aggressively in the international markets.

An international agreement between central banking authorities, known as the Basle Rules or Basle Agreement, was reached in December 1987. The central banks are members of the Bank for International Settlements (BIS), and the agreement also is referred to as the BIS Agreement. Its aims were to apply a common set of rules for capital adequacy to all banks in international banking, and thereby prevent some banks having unfair advantages over others. The agreement was adopted by many countries. For example, it was adopted by the European Union, in a Capital Adequacy Directive.

The agreement contained a minimum risk-asset-ratio requirement and a minimum gearing requirement. It set certain targets or requirements for capital adequacy that all international banks were required to achieve. These targets were as follows:

- A minimum capital:risk-assets ratio of 8%. In other words, a bank's capital must be at least 8% of the risk-weighted value of its assets.

- A minimum core equity:total capital base ratio of 50%. A bank must have at least 50% of its capital as core equity. A bank's capital base consists of Tier 1 and Tier 2 capital. Tier 1 capital is core equity, Tier 2 is not.
- A minimum ratio of core equity to total assets of 4%. This is a minimum gearing requirement.

Tier 1 and Tier 2 Capital

Qualifying capital, i.e. funds that make up a bank's capital base, is divided into two levels or tiers:

- Tier 1 capital, consists of fully paid-up ordinary share capital, non-cumulative perpetual preferred stock and disclosed reserves (retained profits, share premium account, etc.)
- Tier 2 capital, consists of supplementary capital, and includes revaluation reserves, unrealized capital gains on securities owned by the bank, hidden reserves and general provisions. It also includes hybrid debt instruments and subordinated term debt. Subordinated debt only qualifies as Tier 2 capital up to 50% of the amount of Tier 1 capital.

At least 50% of a bank's capital must be Tier 1 capital.

Weighted-Risk Assets

Weightings applied to risk assets are shown in the table on the next page, the list is not complete.

Weighting	Balance sheet items
0%	Cash
	Deposits of the bank with the Central Bank Loans to the domestic central government
	Securities issued by the domestic central government, such as Treasury bills and bonds

Weighting	Balance sheet items (continued)
20%	Claims on other banks with under one year to maturity, i.e. short-term inter-bank loans, etc.
	Claims on other *domestic* banks with an original maturity of one year or more.
50%	Loans fully secured by mortgages, made to owner-occupiers for residential house purchases.
100%	Claims on the private sector, e.g. loans to companies Cross-border claims on banks with an original maturity of over one year
	Premises, plant, equipment, etc.

No attempt was made to usurp the commercial risk assessment of banks. Accordingly, an unsecured loan to a top multinational company attracted the same risk weighting as an unsecured loan to Peter the Plumber. This has been recognized as a weakness in the agreement's rules.

Weighting	Off-balance sheet items
100%	Direct credit substitutes, e.g. guarantees, acceptances, letters of credit as financial guarantees
50%	Transaction-related contingencies, e.g. performance bonds, bid bonds, specific standby letters of credit Other commitments with an original maturity exceeding one year, e.g. standby facilities, credit lines
20%	Short-term, self-liquidating trade-related contingencies, e.g. documentary credits collateralized by shipments

Example

The assets, in sterling, of Epsilon Bank, a UK bank, are listed in the table below. Risk asset values for these assets also are shown.

	Assets £m	Risk weights %	Weighted risk assets £m
Notes, coins, deposits with Bank of England	60	0	0
Treasury bills	80	0	0
Eligible bank bills	200	20	40
Money-market loans	2,500	20	500
Long-term loans			
Central government	100	0	0
Mortgage loans	2,000	50	1,000
Private sector loans	12,000	100	12,000
	16,940		13,540

If off-balance sheet transactions have a weighted-risk asset value of £4,000 million, the bank's total risk-weighted assets would be £17,540 million.

Lending Implications of the Basle Agreement

The capital adequacy requirements have serious implications for the credit capacity of banks because they set a limit on the volume of business a bank can conduct, given the size of its capital base.

Because the rules apply to off-balance sheet transactions, e.g. undrawn facilities, as well as to loans, banks must look closely at the optimal deployment of their scarce capital and focus their business on higher-margin products. Banks must assess the profitability of each of their activities. Non-profit-making activities should be dropped if they cannot be restored to profit. For example, loans to risky customers, where doubtful debt provisions are high, could be curtailed unless the bank can charge a higher margin on the loans. Bank lending, even to investment-grade corporates, has not been one of the higher-margin products. In many cases, even ignoring the cost of bad debt losses, banks have scaled down their corporate lending activity.

Capital adequacy regulations for banks have several implications for companies that wish to borrow.

- *Higher charges.* Banks are likely to make higher charges for services with a higher risk weighting to justify commercially their involvement in such lending activities.
- *Refusal to lend or to offer services.* If a bank's capital base is close to its minimum risk asset ratio, it might refuse to grant extra facilities to a customer, or to sell extra services to which risk weightings would be attached.
- *Withdrawal of lending facilities.* A more serious problem could occur when a bank's capital base is near its minimum risk asset ratio, but the bank is still making losses and its capital base is contracting. In these circumstances, a bank could be forced to cut back its total lending; for example by refusing to renew customers' borrowing facilities. A bank could suddenly reduce a customer's overdraft facility through no fault of the customer.

Target Lending Margins

One impact of the Basle rules is to give banks a better idea of the minimum margin they should make on lending. The margin can be measured as follows:

$$M = \frac{R \times A}{P \times (1 - t)}$$

where M is the required margin on lending

R is the desired after-tax return on equity

A is the target ratio of equity to risk assets

P is the profit margin after deducting administration costs from interest income

t is the rate of tax on profits of the bank, as a proportion.

Example

Epsilon Bank's management consider that shareholders should expect a post-tax return of 15%. The bank is operating at its minimum capital adequacy standard, and the ratio of its equity to risk-weighted assets, i.e. Tier 1 ratio, is 4%. Its profits on lending after deducting operating costs are 50% of revenue, and the rate of tax on profits is 33%.

Analysis

Assuming no bad debts on any loans, the margin required on the bank's lending will be as follows:

$$M = \frac{15 \text{ x } 4}{50 \text{ x } (1 - 0.33)} = 1.8\%$$

The margin must be higher for loans in each credit-risk category to compensate the bank for bad debts on some of its loans to customers in that category.

Commitment Fees

The Basle rules applied a different risk weighting to committed standby facilities compared with term loans. Standby facilities were weighted at only 50% of the total amount of the facility, whereas drawn loans are weighted at 100%.

If a bank must maintain a minimum 8% ratio of capital to weighted risk assets, capital of $8 can support weighted risk assets of $100. These could be a loan of $100 or a committed, but so far unused, standby facility of $200. For the bank to make the same return on standby facilities as for term loans, the front-end fee (the commitment fee) for a facility must be 50% of the fee for a term loan. Banks should adjust their fee structures accordingly.

Capital Adequacy and Provisions for Doubtful Loans

In addition to making banks keenly aware of profit margins on lending, the Basle rules also have made them reconsider their strategy towards lending. Expanding their loan book can be financially harmful if as a consequence there would be a higher level of bad debts.

Losses reduce a bank's capital reserves because they reduce the retained profits of shareholders, and reserves count as Tier 1 capital under the rules. If a bank's capital is already at its minimum level, as a proportion of its total risk-weighted assets, any further losses will have one of two consequences:

- the bank must restore its capital base, perhaps by raising extra equity funds, or by means of long-term borrowing, or
- the bank must reduce its risk-weighted assets, probably by cutting the amount of its lending to customers.

Amending the Capital Adequacy Rules

The Bank for International Settlements has recognized that the original Basle Agreement has significant faults, even though it appears to have been effective on the whole in regulating banks and ensuring capital adequacy in the international banking system. A particular criticism of the old Agreement was that it applied fairly broad and crude controls to lending. Many banks have now developed highly sophisticated risk-monitoring and risk-management models of their own (Value at Risk or VaR models). It has been accepted that approved models could be used by a bank to assess how much it is safe for the bank to lend, and what its minimum level of capital ought to be to support its loan book.

At the time of writing, a new Basle Capital Accord is close to completion, and should be agreed at some time during 2002, with implementation of the new rules by the banking industry in 2005. The delay in implementation is to allow time for the necessary legislative changes, such as a new Capital Adequacy Directive (CAD2) for the European Union.

The main element of the new Accord will be minimum capital

requirements for banks, based on an assessment of both the bank's credit risk and its operational risk.

- Banks will be required to have a minimum amount of capital to cover its credit risks. This is similar to the current regulatory requirement, although some changes will be made to the calculation of a bank's risk-weighted assets and different approaches to the capital adequacy calculations will be allowed.
- In addition, banks will be required to have a minimum amount of capital to cover its operational risks. Operational risk is the risk of losses resulting from failed or inadequate processes, people or systems, or from external events. In the proposed approach to calculating the minimum capital requirement, a risk measure or indicator, expressed as a probability or percentage figure, will be applied to the business lines of each bank. This will be used to calculate a minimum capital requirement for operations of the bank, such as corporate finance business, trading and sales, retail banking, commercial banking, payments and settlement, retail brokerage and asset management.

Securitization of Assets (Asset-Backed Securities)

The desire by banks to reduce their loan book, or keep lending under control, has resulted in an expansion in the market for asset-backed securities and the securitization of banking assets.

A bank can take loans, e.g. mortgage loans, off its balance sheet by setting up a separate company known as a special-purpose vehicle or SPV, to whom the bank can sell its loans. The SPV can package the loans into securities, such as bonds or commercial paper, and sell these to investors. The interest payments and eventual repayment of principal to the investors will come from the proceeds of the mortgages or other financial assets that back the securities.

10

Negotiating Bank Loans and Facilities

In negotiating a loan, a company is entering into a business contract with its bank. No matter how good the relationship between them might be, each has its own interests to consider. Each side must decide what it wants from the loan agreement and how much it is willing to concede in negotiation. All business arrangements are best built on mutual understanding, respect and trust. Deals should satisfy both parties and be mutually beneficial.

Stages in Negotiating a Loan or Facility

The stages in the negotiation process are:

- the initial approach to a bank by the company
- a credit-risk assessment of the company by the bank
- an initial offer from the bank, in a term sheet
- further discussion of terms, e.g. price, term, loan structure, security and covenants
- agreement and documentation.

Stages in Arranging a Loan

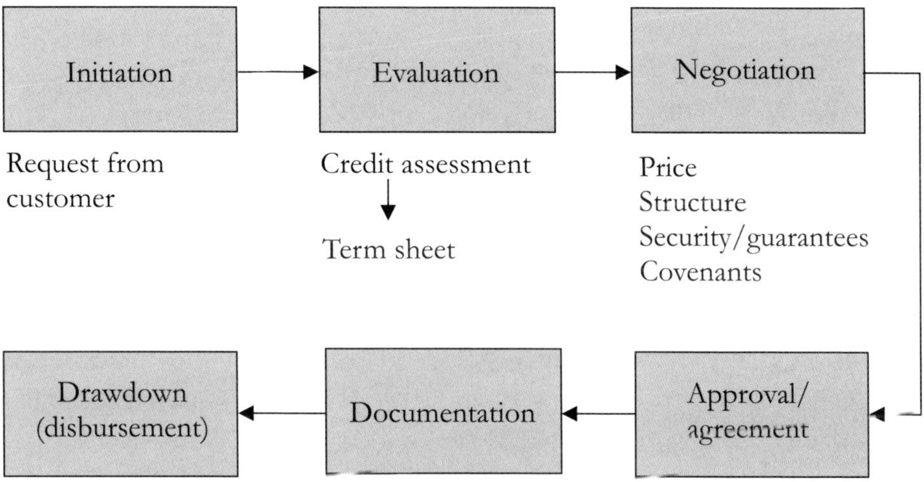

A loan agreement is a contract between the lending bank and the borrower and the same criteria apply as when negotiating a loan (see introductory paragraph to this chapter).

The stages in a loan negotiation process are:

- the initial approach, usually by the company to a bank
- a credit assessment of the company by the bank and credit clearance from the bank's credit committee or credit department
- an initial offer from the bank to the customer, set out in a term sheet
- discussion of terms in detail, e.g. interest rate, fees, security and covenants
- agreement and loan documentation.

Credit Approval

When a company and a bank begin to discuss a loan facility, they might come to a general view on what type of loan facility the customer needs, for how much and for how long. Before detailed negotiations can begin, the transaction will go through a credit-approval process by the bank. Every lending bank has specialist credit analysts, who carry out checks on a customer to decide whether the bank should be prepared to lend money, and if so, how much.

A bank will not lend money without carrying out an investigation into the borrower and the purpose of the loan. The scale and depth of these investigations will depend on the extent to which the bank already knows the customer, and the size of the proposed loan or facility. Very careful checking will be carried out for a new customer, and for an unusually large lending proposal from an established customer.

Credit checks are carried out to assess the likelihood that the borrower will be able to afford the interest payments (service the loan) and make the capital repayment. Depending on how the borrower and the loan proposal is assessed, the bank will decide either to refuse or agree to the loan, and if it agrees, at what interest rate, at what margin above LIBOR or base rate.

This fact-finding and credit assessment exercise is referred to as due diligence. The purpose of due diligence is to assess the credit risk for the bank, so that the bank:

- will not undertake lending that it considers insufficiently profitable for the risk involved, and
- will not take on a portfolio of loans that exposes the bank to risks of severe losses due to default, for example in the event of a downturn in the economy, or in a particular industry.

Banks will consider individual loans within the context of their overall loans position, not just on the merits of the individual loan proposal.

Credit Analysis

The loan proposal will be analysed by credit analysts who will be looking for evidence of the company's ability to repay any loan. The checks will include an analysis of the company's accounts, including:

- its most recent annual report and accounts
- if there are any, more recent interim (half-year) accounts
- in some cases, more recent internal management accounts of the company.

The ability of a bank's credit department to obtain management accounts from a company will depend on the balance of power between the company and the bank. Very large companies might refuse to provide any information to the bank that is not already in the public domain, and threaten to go to another bank for a loan if the bank insists on having more information. In contrast, a bank might be able to demand detailed management accounting information from a smaller company, with the threat of refusing to lend if it doesn't get the information it is requesting.

At the end of their investigation, the credit analysts will prepare a report on the company's creditworthiness and on the loan proposal.

Credit Clearance

Loan proposals are submitted to an appropriate level of management within the bank for approval (credit clearance). The bank will have a credit committee, or similar decision-making body, that considers all loan proposals, and the accompanying report from the credit analysts.

The credit committee will consider the loan and also the broader strategic picture of the bank's overall lending position. A commercial bank has a portfolio of many different loans. If a bank has a large proportion of loans to one particular type of customer, for example to customers in the same industry or to customers in a particular geographical area, it might consider itself over-exposed to the risk of a downturn in financial or economic conditions among those customers. For example:

- a bank with a large quantity of loans to customers in Brazil would be particularly exposed to the risk of a downturn in the Brazilian economy

- a bank with a large quantity of loans to dot.com companies will be exposed to a recession in the e-commerce industry.

A bank will have an overall credit policy, and will wish to ensure that external constraints such as its capital-adequacy requirements, and internal policy constraints are not breached.

The credit committee will reach its decision and:

- reject the loan proposal
- approve (clear) the loan proposal as submitted
- clear the proposal, but subject to certain conditions such as insisting on the inclusion of a particular loan covenant in the loan agreement, or reducing the total size of the loan.

Once a loan proposal has been cleared by the credit committee, the account officer will draw up a term sheet.

Term Sheet

A term sheet is a document that sets out the main terms for a proposed lending transaction. It is prepared by the bank and sent to the prospective borrower for acceptance. A term sheet is not intended as a legally binding document. Signing it simply indicates the company's acceptance of the broad terms, and a willingness to move on to the next stage of the loan negotiations, but although a term sheet is not intended as a legally binding document, it has a moral authority. If the company accepts its terms, both it and the bank are giving a moral undertaking to proceed with the negotiations in good faith, on the understanding that they both intend to work towards reaching an agreement.

The purpose of the term sheet is to set down the main terms of the proposed lending arrangement, but without going into excessive detail. The structure and contents of a term sheet will vary with the bank and according to the type of loan or facility. An example of the main contents of a typical term sheet is shown opposite.

TERM SHEET (SUBJECT TO CONTRACT)

	Name of borrower and name of lender.
Facility	Amount and type of facility, e.g. $30 million term loan.
Commitment fee	Any commitment fee, and if so, the amount and frequency of payment.
Purpose of loan	In broad outline only, what the borrower intends to do with the money.
Availability	The period of time after the signing of the loan documentation during which the loan will be available for draw down by the customer, i.e. during which the funds will be available to borrow.
Interest rate payable	Amount and frequency of payments, e.g. LIBOR plus 110 basis points, payable at the end of every three months.
Maturity/term	Number of years to maturity, and from what date, e.g. seven years from the date of the signing of the loan documentation.
Repayment of loan capital	Details of how the loan capital will be repaid, for example in a bullet repayment at maturity or by amortization over the term of the loan. A schedule for the loan capital repayments will be specified for balloon repayment.
Early repayment of loan capital	If the loan agreement provides for the early repayment of the loan capital, the conditions under which this may be done should be specified.

TERM SHEET (SUBJECT TO CONTRACT) (cont.)	
Security	Broad details of the security to be provided by the borrower.
Conditions precedent	The term sheet will specify the conditions that must be fulfilled by the borrower before the loan will be made. For example, the customer must pay the arrangement fee/bank's expenses in advance.
Representations and warranties	The term sheet might state that the usual representations and warranties will be required from the borrower. Any unusual representations and warranties should be specified.
Covenants	The term sheet might state that the borrower will give the standard covenants, 'including but not limited to…', followed by a list of covenants. Financial covenants might be explained more specifically. Any unusual covenants should be specified.
Events of default	The term sheet might state that there will be the usual events of default, 'including but not limited to…' followed by an indicative list.
Taxes	There may be a statement that the interest payments will be made by the borrower free from any withholding tax or other taxes.
Costs	The bank will require the borrower to undertake to pay certain expenses and costs, such as solicitors' fees. By accepting the term sheet, the borrower will be

TERM SHEET (SUBJECT TO CONTRACT) (cont.)	
	committed to paying those costs. There must be a provision in the term sheet whereby the customer gives this undertaking, whether or not a loan agreement is reached.
Confidentiality	The term sheet may include a confidentiality undertaking by the bank, or a statement that the bank will provide a confidentiality letter if the company accepts the term sheet. The binding nature of the bank's undertaking should be made clear.
Assignment	The bank has the right to assign all or part of the loan or facility at any time.

Lending Terms

After the term sheet has been prepared, the terms of the agreement will be negotiated in further detail, and the loan agreement document will be drafted. The main terms in the loan agreement that can be discussed before the agreement is finalized, relate to:

- price
- structure
- security and guarantees
- covenants
- provisions for transfers or assignments

The negotiation on pricing should take place first because the price should influence the discussions about the other lending terms, particularly the loan covenants.

Price

Bank pricing takes account of several factors:

- the perceived credit risk of the borrower
- the current market rate for similar facilities of similar credit risk
- the strength of the bargaining positions of the bank and the customer
- the appetite of the bank for lending – a function of its capital base, financial health and lending policy.

A combination of these factors produces a pricing range for loans that, including front-end and commitment/facility fees, for a large company could be 50 to 150 basis points (1.00-1.50%) over LIBOR over the life of the loan. The comparable range for a small business might be base rate plus 3-7%, or even more. A company's finance director or treasurer can guess at the limits of this range using recent experience, knowledge of the pricing of similar transactions and conversations with one or more bankers.

The bank's initial offer on pricing usually is negotiable, even for small companies. However a company is unlikely to extract a big change from the prices contained in the term sheet. For example, if a bank quotes a drawing margin on a floating-rate facility of LIBOR plus 200 basis points, a corporate borrower would be wasting its time to counter-propose a significantly different rate, for example LIBOR plus 0.50%. It might be possible to negotiate a reduction of up to 25 basis points from this price.

The most effective approach to negotiating price is to concentrate on the most significant element. In the case of a standby facility for contingency funding that has a low likelihood of being drawn, the company should concentrate its efforts on negotiating a reduction in the commitment fee. Conversely, if the intention is to draw heavily upon a facility, the drawing margin (interest rate) should be the primary focus of negotiations.

A company gets only one opportunity to ask the bank to adjust its pricing so it is important to establish:

- an optimum target price
- the prices that it would be prepared to accept, and
- the particular area(s) of pricing that are most significant for the negotiations.

Fixed or Floating Rate?

The company must indicate whether it would like to borrow at a fixed or at a floating rate. The cost of floating-rate funds reflects market interest rates. The rate for a fixed-rate loan to a large company is based on the cost of government debt. Companies borrow at a margin over the rate paid by the sovereign borrower. The size of this margin will reflect the particular company's credit rating or, if unrated, its perceived credit standing. A Triple A-rated company with the highest corporate credit rating could borrow at 20 basis points (0.20%) over the government rate for a fixed period of two years or 65 basis points (0.65%) over the government rate for a ten-year loan. The equivalent rates for a less highly rated but creditworthy company with a single-A rating could be a 30 basis points margin at two years and 110 basis points margin at ten years.

In practise, even the largest companies will find it difficult, if not impossible, to borrow fixed-rate money from their banks for a period in excess of ten years. Small companies will experience similar difficulties when looking for fixed-rate money for a term in excess of five years.

A small company also will have difficulty identifying a benchmark rate of interest against which to judge the fixed-interest rate quoted by its bank for a term loan. This is because there will be a high margin for credit risk that the company has no means of assessing objectively, for example, against a formal credit rating. The margins quoted by banks for fixed-rate loans to small companies could be between 500 and 700 basis points or higher over the gilts rate. Even so, a small company should measure the cost of its fixed-rate borrowings against the benchmark of the cost of government debt for the same maturity.

Some companies might choose to borrow from a bank at a floating rate, and then arrange an interest rate swap. This would have the effect of changing the variable-rate payments on the loan to fixed-rate payments on the loan and swap combined. The details of interest-rate swaps are outside the scope of this book.

Tax Gross-up Clause

A loan agreement could include a tax gross-up clause that provides for a higher rate of interest to be paid if the borrower has to make a deduction for tax, i.e. if there is withholding tax on interest payments.

A withholding tax is a tax deducted at source and paid to the government. For example, suppose that a US company borrows from a foreign bank at 9%. If there is withholding tax of 10% on interest payments from the US to the bank's country, the company would pay interest of just 8.1% (9% – 0.9% tax) to the bank, and withholding tax of 0.9% (10% of 9%) to the UK government. The bank would receive less in interest than the company pays because of the tax deduction.

If a tax gross-up clause were to be introduced, the company would be required to pay 9% net of tax to the bank, and its gross interest payment would be 10% (tax would be 1%).

Structure

Negotiations could be necessary about the structure of the proposed loan or facility. The bank and the company could have differing views about whether a loan or a facility would be appropriate, what the repayment profile for a loan should be and whether a facility should be committed or uncommitted. Major banks can accommodate almost any structure that a company wishes but they are by no means always willing to agree to an irregular structure. The term of the loan or facility also must be agreed.

Repayment Profile

A loan involving irregular principal payments usually will cost a few basis points more than a plain vanilla amortizing loan with equal repayments of principal. Unusual structures can include:

- an irregular pattern of debt repayment to match the cash flow of the project and business – a sawtooth pattern
- a principal repayment holiday at the start of the loan until the positive cash flow builds up, e.g. loans for long-term construction
- deferral of interest payments for part or all of the loan – an interest payment holiday

A company should evaluate the comparative cost of:

- a standard plain vanilla repayment structure, with which there could be an imperfect match between the borrower's cash flows and the loan repayment pattern, and
- a customized structure that provides perfectly matched fundings.

Early Repayment Provision

Floating-rate loans normally allow the borrower the option of early repayment, with little or no penalty, but there can be significant costs for early repayment of fixed-rate loans if interest rates have fallen since the initial drawdown. A company should try to achieve flexibility by having a provision in the agreement for early repayment at any time, ideally without penalty, particularly in the case of floating-rate loans.

Term Loan or Facility?

A borrower, particularly a smaller company, should try to negotiate a term loan rather than a revolving credit facility. The borrower would have to draw down the full amount of the loan from the outset and pay interest on this over the term of the loan. However, it would be in a stronger position if it were to breach any covenant. The bank could refuse further lending on a revolving facility when an event of default occurs, and perhaps force the company into liquidation. A term loan would not allow the bank to do this. It would have to hope that in spite of the covenant breach, the borrower would pay its loan obligations in full.

Security and Guarantees

The borrower should not agree lightly to any demands by the bank for security or guarantees. An agreement to give security should, where possible, be in exchange for a lower rate of interest.

Negotiations between the borrower and the bank on pricing should include discussions about the security the borrower can offer the lender, or guarantees that can be provided.

The bank might indicate a preference for a guarantee, but would be willing to give a loan without security or guarantee. In this situation, the borrower should ask the bank what the pricing benefit for conceding the guarantee would be, compared with the price for an unguaranteed loan. The difference between the interest rate for unguaranteed project finance and for guaranteed borrowing could be as much as 500 basis points or even more.

Lending to Group Companies

A bank can be asked to lend to a company within a group. Groups can be a particular problem for a lending bank, because:

- the borrowing company could have relatively few assets to offer as security, although the group as a whole could be large
- subsidiaries and sub-subsidiaries, etc., can be located in several countries
- cash flows between companies in the group can be complex.

In a large group the parent company could be a holding company whose only assets are its investments in subsidiary companies. When the parent company wants to borrow, for example to finance another investment, the lending bank could ask for an upstream guarantee. This is a guarantee from a subsidiary in support of a bank loan to the parent company. The subsidiary would have to have sufficient tangible assets to give substance to the guarantee.

There is a benefit from taking upstream guarantees. In the event of a liquidation of the group, the bank would rank pari passu, in the hierarchy of right to payment, along with the unsecured creditors of the subsidiary giving the guarantee. Without the upstream guarantee, the bank would have to seek payment from the residual assets of the holding company, after the claims of its subsidiaries' creditors had been met in full.

Upstream guarantees from subsidiaries are reinforced by cross-stream guarantees between the subsidiaries. The bank's aim should be to ensure that if the guarantee has to be enforced, the bank can claim against the assets of the group.

Example
Able Limited, a subsidiary of the Sierra Group, is seeking a loan from its bank. The bank is willing to lend, but wants suitable security or guarantees. Sierra Group has the following group structure.

Sierra Group Structure

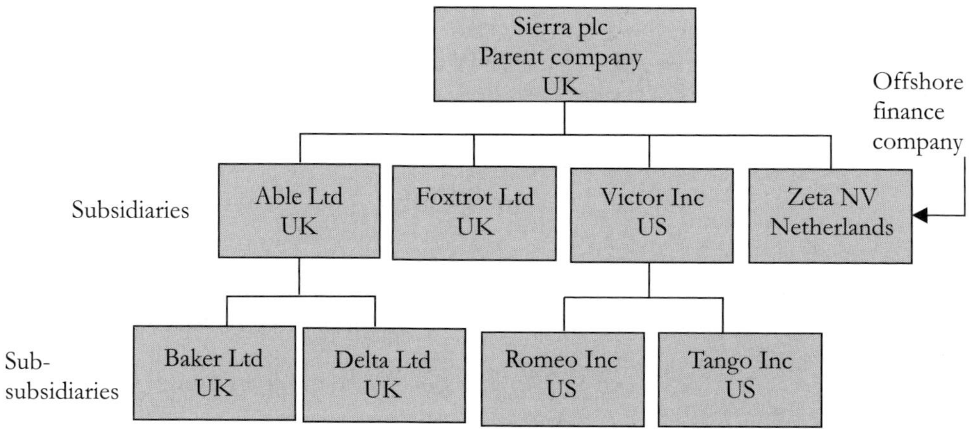

Analysis
If a UK bank were asked to lend to the group, the borrower probably would be one of the UK companies. The bank might be willing to lend, satisfied that the borrower's cash flows should be sufficient to repay the loan on schedule, but would also want security or a guarantee or several guarantees.

If Able has valuable assets, the bank could ask for the loan to be secured by a charge on those assets. If the borrower is not asset-rich, the bank should seek guarantees from other group companies. The bank would want a guarantee from the parent company, Sierra plc (a downstream guarantee) and possibly from Foxtrot, the other UK subsidiary in the group (a cross-stream guarantee).

Covenants

The negotiation of covenants can be as crucial as negotiations on pricing. The bank should look to limit the credit risk. The borrower's management should try to concede as few restrictions as possible, to retain their flexibility to run the business without being excessively constrained by loan covenants.

A borrower must recognize the need for its bank(s) to have adequate comfort. The end-result of negotiations on covenants should be a happy medium between quantitative covenants that give such comfort to the bank yet allow the borrower sufficient operational flexibility. If the bank is concerned about a lack of protection from the covenants, it will expect the borrower to pay a higher price for the loan.

A bank will try to insist that a loan agreement includes:

- a negative pledge
- a cross-default clause
- a material adverse change clause, and
- a small number of suitable quantitative covenants.

When quantitative covenants are negotiated, it is essential for the bank and the borrower to work through the detail with care. Definitions of financial ratios and the method of valuation for particular types of asset could be crucially important. For example, it could be important to agree on whether the minority shareholders' interest within a group of companies should be included in the valuation of the group's net worth.

Example
Delta has the following balance sheet.

	$m
Tangible fixed assets	40
Intangible fixed assets	8
Net current assets	12
	60
Loans (excluding convertibles)	15
	45
Ordinary share capital	10
Reserves	30
Total equity	40
Convertible loan stock	5
	45

In negotiations for a new loan agreement, Delta's bank wants to have a minimum net-worth covenant. Before agreeing to such a covenant, and deciding the minimum amount, Delta and the bank must agree how net worth should be defined. Using current balance-sheet valuations, the net worth of Delta could be:

- as high as $45 million, if equity includes convertible loan stock and intangible fixed assets are assumed to have value, or
- as low as $32 million ($40 million – $8 million), if equity

excludes convertible loan stock, and intangible fixed assets are assumed to have no worth.

Frozen GAAP and Rolling GAAP

The problem of measurement is further complicated by the fact that accounting practises change. Methods of measuring asset values and profits are different now from those used just a few years ago.

Changes in generally accepted accounting procedures, or GAAP for short, can have implications for loan covenants. For example, suppose that a company accepted a covenant in a five-year loan that its interest cover ratio would not fall below 3.5 times. Suppose also that in the second year of the loan, its interest costs were $5 million and its reported profit would have been $18 million, if accounting procedures were used that had been the GAAP when the loan was made. However, new accounting regulations have been introduced and using the new GAAP, its profit in the second year would have been just $15 million for example.

It could be argued that the company is in breach of its interest cover covenant because cover is only 3.0 times (15 million ÷ 5 million). On the other hand, it could be argued also that the company has kept within its covenant, measuring profit by the old rules because 18 million ÷ 5 million gives a cover of 3.6 times.

The issue illustrated here is that in agreeing loan covenants, it must be established whether financial measurements will use:

- the accounting rules applying at the start of the loan term – frozen GAAP, or
- the accounting rules that currently apply – rolling GAAP.

Research has indicated that in the past, most loan contracts made use of rolling GAAP, putting borrowers at risk of breaching loan covenants because of a change in accounting rules, not because of any unforeseen change in their financial circumstances.

Dangers Arising from Specific Covenants

To determine just what covenants it is appropriate to concede, the borrowing company must try to foresee the future development and shape of its business during the projected life of the loan. It is essential to know whether the business could be in a cycle of downturn or upturn, and to understand how vulnerable or volatile its profitability might be. There could be particular dangers with three covenants, and a borrower would be well advised either to avoid them if possible or to negotiate their wording carefully. The three covenants are:

- an interest cover test
- a material adverse change clause, and
- a cross-default clause.

Risk from an Interest Cover Test

It can be very risky for a company with vulnerable earnings to concede an interest cover test. If it were to suffer a fall in profits, a breach of the covenant could deliver the company into the hands of its bankers. This could occur despite the fact that the company might be profitable over the long term.

Risk from a Material Adverse Change Clause

A material adverse change clause can be even more dangerous to corporate health. Unlike an interest cover covenant, it is a qualitative (unquantified) covenant under which an event of default is based purely on the bank's judgment. In the likely event that the bank will take a different view from the borrower, the bank can demand immediate repayment of a term loan, or prevent the borrower drawing further on a committed facility. The bank need not then be in a hurry to settle the argument about whether or not a material adverse change has taken place.

This situation can deliver even a modestly geared company into the hands of its bankers when it has a pressing need for further funds or when other outstanding loans have a cross-default clause. The company would have to redeem the debt quickly to avoid cross-default on its other loan agreements, and it would need funds from some other source in order to do this.

The typical wording of a material adverse change clause states that an event of default will occur if any event or circumstance arises that the bank determines will or may have a material adverse effect on the condition of the borrower or its willingness or ability to perform or comply with any one or more of its obligations under this agreement.

Companies that are a low credit risk should be able to persuade their bank to exclude such a clause on the grounds that other quantitative financial covenants will provide sufficient credit protection for the bank.

If a company is unable to persuade its bank to drop this covenant from the loan agreement, it should seek to restrict the covenant and narrow its scope to events that affect the ability of the borrower to fulfill its payment obligations. A corporate borrower would prefer a covenant in which a material adverse change is defined as any event or circumstance arising that will have a material adverse effect on the borrower's ability to perform or comply with its payment obligations under this agreement. This wording differs from the typical wording shown above because it excludes any reference either to the bank's judgment of what may happen, or to the general condition of the borrower. It focuses on the borrower's ability to repay the loan.

Risk from a Cross-Default Clause

Banks often will insist on a cross-default clause as a non-negotiable condition of a loan. A default on any other loan would trigger an event of default on the loan with a cross-default clause.

The most restrictive set of covenants conceded by the company in any of its loan agreements apply by proxy to all its other loan agreements if these include a cross-default clause. In effect, the lowest common denominator, in covenant terms, sets the level of protection from covenants that are enjoyed by every lender with cross-default rights.

It is important to check the potential consequences of any cross-default clause. Non-payment of a trade bill, for example, should not be an event of default arising from a cross-default clause being triggered.

A Borrower's Strategy on Covenants

A large company that is likely to have multiple-loan agreements is best advised to formulate and insist upon a standard set of loan covenants. These covenants should be framed in consultation with one or more of the company's relationship banks to ensure that they meet the twin aims of:

- providing sufficient operating flexibility for the company, and
- giving the lender adequate comfort about the financial position of the borrower.

It should then be possible to offer the standard set of covenants on a non-negotiable basis to banks for all future loan transactions. Large companies with strong financial muscle are clearly in a better position than small companies to negotiate covenants in this way.

Advantages of a Standard Set of Covenants

A standard set of covenants has some clear advantages for a corporate borrower.

- It provides consistency throughout all the company's loan agreements.
- It calls for consistency of treatment of all relationship banks by the borrower. Banks often are less concerned about winning preferential treatment over other lenders and are more concerned about ensuring that other lenders do not receive preferential treatment over them.
- Covenants can be monitored more easily because the same covenants apply to all loans.
- Because there is no negotiation on one-off (customized) covenants, there will be lower legal fees for arranging the loan agreement.
- The problem with cross-default clauses, referred to above, would not apply.

Non-Standard (Customized) Covenants

In the event that a borrower opts for – or the bank insists on –

customized rather than standardized covenants, the onus should be on the company to decide:

- which covenants it will not accept under any circumstances
- which covenants it would prefer not to concede, but would be prepared to do so if necessary to secure the transaction
- the acceptable levels for any quantified covenants that the company is prepared to concede.

The company must state its views to the bank, preferably at a face-to-face meeting rather than in writing. It should emphasize which covenants are non-negotiable and indicate its position on covenants that it is willing to concede. The response of the bank could depend on the strength of the relationship between bank and borrower.

Provisions for Transfer or Assignment

A company might wish to consider its negotiating position on the bank's right to transfer or assign the loan or facility without prior consent from the company.

If the company insists on a blanket prohibition on transfer or assignment, the bank could justifiably insist on a higher rate of interest as compensation for its greater credit exposure to the borrower.

Compromise solutions can be negotiated. For example, a borrower could insist that any transfer should be to a bank from a particular safe jurisdiction or that transfers should be limited to no more than a specified number of banks.

If the company were unable to negotiate as many concessions on transfers as it would like, it could try to insist on prior notice of transfer or assignment. This would give the company an opportunity to object to any particular transfer before it happened even though the bank could choose to ignore the objection and make the transfer anyway.

In addition, the company could insist on linking the bank's

confidentiality undertaking to the transfer provision, so that the bank could not pass on confidential information about the company to another bank, i.e. prior to agreeing a transfer with that bank, without the company's consent.

Syndicated Lending and Sub-Participation

Syndicated lending requires that the borrower should negotiate hard on the composition of the banks in the syndicate. For example, it can insist on including banks with which it already has some dealing relationship, and on excluding banks that have a reputation for quickly transferring their part of the facility to other banks.

Small Companies

Small companies, in terms of banking relationships, could be public companies with a market capitalization of up to $150 million. They could be in a weak bargaining position with their bank and could have difficulty in persuading the bank to alter any lending terms and conditions. This is particularly true for a company that relies heavily on one bank for its external financing, often in the form of an overdraft facility secured by a fixed and floating charge over the the company's assets, and often with a personal guarantee from the major shareholders. Key-man insurance also might be required to protect the bank from the consequences of debilitating injury to, or the death of, an individual on whom the company depends as its main driving force.

Bank-Funding Options for a Company

A small company has considerably less latitude in negotiating bank funding than medium-sized and large companies. The restrictions on their options are suggested in the list below.

- Term. The bank will be reluctant to commit loan finance beyond a five-year period.

- Principal repayment. It is likely that that bank will limit the company's option on principal repayment to a bullet or an amortizing repayment with a strong preference for the latter.
- Interest-rate basis. The bank will favor a floating-rate lending rather than a fixed-rate loan. In addition it would be difficult, if not impossible, for a small company to change the interest basis from floating to fixed by means of a swap or forward rate agreement (FRA) because of the small size of the loan.
- Loan or committed facility. The bank will favor either a fully drawn term loan, or if a facility is required, an uncommitted overdraft facility. It might be reluctant to grant a small corporate borrower a committed overdraft facility or revolving credit facility.
- Bilateral or syndicated loan. A small company will have to raise finance with one bank or several banks on a bilateral basis.
- Secured or unsecured borrowing. The bank will look for specific security or a floating charge over the company's assets and perhaps personal guarantees from its directors. Unsecured lending is fairly normal for large companies, but not for small companies.

These restrictions on borrowing flexibility are due to the size of the company and the funds involved, the generally higher default risk for small companies and the strength of the negotiating position of the banks.

Documentation

A loan agreement will be documented. In the case of large loans, the documentation will specify the amount, maturity, price and repayment details, together with specifications about other loan terms, such as covenants, security and guarantees, events of default, rights of transfer of loans, and early repayment provisions.

Banking Relationships. Monitoring Loans

A distinction can be made between relationship banking and transactions banking. A company wanting banking services can use a bank with which it has a good and regular relationship (relationship banking) or it can ask several banks to quote for a particular transaction and choose the most favorable quote (transactions banking).

A bank can use both approaches to customers. It will try to protect its business with existing customers and appoint bank liaison officers to take care of the relationship. At the same time, its product sales staff can try to sell products and transactions to other companies with which the bank does not have an established relationship.

Transactions and Relationship Banking Approaches

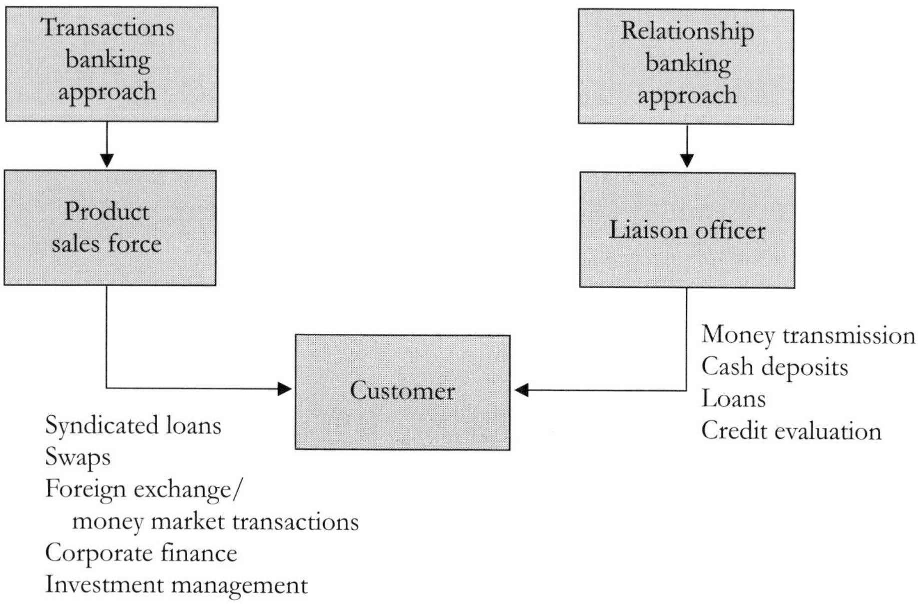

Transactions Banking or Relationship Banking?

For any particular service, the corporate customer can select between dealing with a relationship bank or a transactions bank.

The most common form of corporate lending is a one-to-one (bilateral) arrangement between the company and a bank of its choice. This is usually the company's house bank that also manages its bank accounts and money transmission. A small company, or a larger company that does not have heavy borrowing requirements, is likely to prefer the convenience of this type of relationship.

When such a company wants to borrow, it is unlikely to ask for a price quotation from any other bank; rather it will trust its house bank to charge a fair price. Another bank could be approached if the house bank's quoted price seemed unusually high.

For companies with large borrowing requirements, the choice between a relationship-banking and a transactions-banking approach can be a more difficult one to make. There are two reasons for this difficulty:

- cost, and
- the size of the borrowing requirement.

When banks are willing to lend, and are competing for business, a transactions banking approach should secure cheaper borrowing rates. In a syndicated facility, banks in a syndicate will quote for business and the customer can select the cheapest prices. A saving of just ten basis points (0.10%), for example, on a loan of $100 million would save the company $100,000 each year.

However, a company should be aware that pursuing the finest prices can lead to a reduced level of service from its banks because it wouldn't be worthwhile for the banks to offer anything better.

For large borrowing requirements, a single bank often will be unwilling to lend the full amount because of the large credit exposure to the customer it would create. A bank could be willing to provide funds, but only on condition that the customer will agree to the bank selling on a large part of the loan or facility through transfer, assignment or sub-participation.

Monitoring Loans

The relationship between a corporate borrower and a lending bank does not cease once the company and the bank have signed the loan agreement and the funds have been drawn. The loan documentation almost certainly will impose an ongoing duty on the company to provide progress reports to the bank. In addition to this formal requirement, there is also an informal requirement for the company to ensure that its relationship with the bank remains good, so that the company will be more likely to obtain further help from the bank in the future, should it ever be needed. The cornerstone of a sound borrowing/lending relationship is communication and information.

Managing this relationship can be described as the aftercare of a loan agreement. It should take a number of forms:

- timely payment of debt servicing obligations
- progress reports on the borrower's state of financial health
- monitoring the borrower's position with respect to the loan covenants
- refinancing, if required, as maturity approaches.

Payment of Debt Servicing Obligations

The borrower must ensure that payments of interest and principal payments are made in full on the due dates. At the start of the term for a fixed-rate loan, the bank will provide a schedule showing the precise amount and due date of each payment over the full life of the loan. Sometimes banks will agree to send a reminder in advance of each due payment, but the responsibility for making the payment promptly rests with the borrower.

A floating-rate loan will have the interest rate fixed at the start of each interest period (each rollover period) with the interest payment at the end of the period. The lending bank will notify the company at each reset date of the new interest rate that applies, and the amount of the next loan repayment.

For a committed facility, there is a regular quarterly or bi-annual commitment fee. Payment reminders can be sent out in advance by the bank. Interest on short-term drawings under a committed facility is paid on the maturity of each specific drawing.

Most loan agreements allow a grace period during which an overdue payment can be made before the non-payment ranks as an event of default. Banks will notify a company of the non-payment to ensure that the situation is rectified quickly.

In the case of a small company the principal, interest and other fees payable are deducted automatically from the company's account with the bank.

Computerized cash-management systems often include a diary function that allows the customer to enter instructions for future payments as far forward as required, and then produces daily or weekly listings of forthcoming payments as an aide memoire.

Progress Reports on the Borrower's Financial Health

Most often it is a contractual requirement for a corporate borrower to provide the lender with copies of each set of accounts published by the company during the term of a loan or facility. Some loan agreements go further and call for more regular information, such as monthly management accounts and a copy of all public announcements and press releases made by the company. If the borrower is in a weak negotiating position with its bank, it will have to agree to supply whatever information the bank requests.

Although it is rarely a formal requirement, it is sound business practise for a company to arrange regular meetings with its lenders. These meetings could be arranged annually, unless the company's financial health dictates more frequent contact.

Monitoring Covenants

A company has an ongoing requirement to monitor its adherence to its loan covenants for as long as the loans are outstanding. The standard form of loan documentation requires that a company should notify the bank immediately if it believes that a breach of covenant has taken place. Lenders also have the right to call for an independent assessment of the company's adherence to its covenants. It is a useful discipline for a company to calculate its position with respect to quantitative covenants every time it prepares financial accounts that could be every month.

When there is an actual or prospective breach of covenant, control of the company effectively is handed over to the banks. In cases where banks have forced a company into liquidation, the bank's decision often has been triggered by a breach of covenant, and a judgment that the company's financial position cannot be improved.

A breach of covenant does not necessarily lead to the demise of the company. Many businesses suffer a technical breach of covenant where a minor infringement has taken place. Provided the company management can convince the bank of its intention to rectify the breach within an acceptable period, a waiver will be granted, excusing that specific breach from event-of-default status. Some syndicated banking agreements insist on unanimity among the lending syndicate before such a waiver can be granted. It is preferable to structure a syndicated agreement to allow for a waiver by a majority decision of the syndicate banks to reduce the scope for one or two banks to wield a disproportionate amount of power on waiver negotiations.

Aftercare

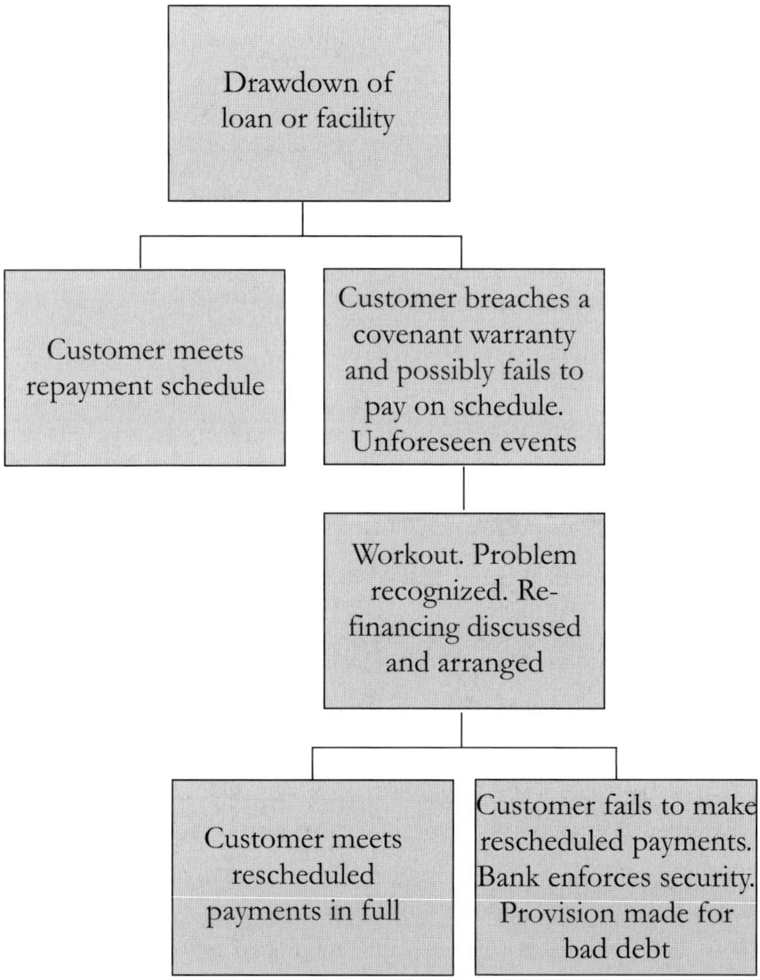

Refinancing

When a company is funded by medium or long-term loans, often it will need to renew the loans when they mature to obtain on-going finance.

The company's management has two courses of action:

- to try to refinance on more advantageous terms during the life of the current loan (interim refinance), or

- to arrange refinance if required on maturity of the loan.

Interim Refinance
Opportunities can arise during the term of a loan for a company to refinance its funding requirements on better terms than the current loan. This can occur for example when the borrower's creditworthiness improves from the time of arranging the original loan. If this improvement is significant it could benefit the company to repay the original loan and negotiate a replacement loan at a new lower margin.

Refinancing on Maturity of a Loan
A company either can repay a maturing loan out of its own cash resources, that is out of the cash flows generated by the project or business requiring the initial finance, or by borrowing again and using the loan proceeds to repay the old loan.

It can take up to three months to renegotiate a bank loan and because a bank might refuse to lend, forcing the company to start fresh negotiations with other banks, it is advisable to start the refinancing negotiation several months prior to maturity of the original loan.

A company will start by asking the bank that is providing the current loan to provide the refinancing. This should reduce the amount of work at the company and at the bank because there is a good chance that the existing form of loan agreement can be applied to the follow-on loan. If so, there would be administrative and legal savings for the bank and the company. Because credit approval for the previous loan is already in place, the renewal simply should require ratification by the bank's credit committee rather than a fundamental credit appraisal. The company should be aware of how market pricing and covenant practise might have altered between the time of the original loan agreement and the time of renewal. If prices have risen, for example, if bank margins are higher, or if covenant requirements have been tightened, the bank will attempt to apply these to the new loan. If prices have fallen, or new-loan covenant requirements are now less arduous, the bank could try to renew on the existing terms, and the company should be ready to argue the point.

Forced Mid-Term Refinancing

Heavily indebted companies could be unable to pay their debt obligations in the short term, even though they could be financially viable in the long term. Their problem is short-term liquidity (cash flow) rather than long-term profitability. If an event of default, such as failure to make an interest payment, or an actual or potential breach of covenant forces a company to negotiate a refinancing package with its bank(s), the company is in a very weak negotiating position.

Banks are fully aware of their responsibilities in supporting ailing companies and know that continued financial support to a company can offer the best opportunity to recover their loans. A bank could take the view that if, in its opinion, a borrower falls into this category, it would be appropriate to provide continuing financial support. This would be in the bank's interest as well as the borrower's, because a bad debt loss could be avoided.

Continuing bank support could take the form of a larger facility, a new loan, or extending the term of an existing loan.

A bank will seek four concessions from a company in a rescue refinancing negotiation:

- Substantial front-end fees, between 1% and 5%, of the refinancing amount.
- Substantially higher pricing for the drawing margin above base rate or LIBOR for facilities and term loans.
- Security for the new loans.
- A detailed business plan from management for trading the company out of trouble, or raising cash to repay some of its loans by selling off parts of its business.

In return for these concessions the banks will, if they see a good prospect for the company's survival and improvement in profits and cash flow, commit the necessary amount of capital, reschedule the debt repayments and adjust the quantitative loan covenants to a level consistent with the new business plan that should not trigger an event of default. They will, however, set the revised quantitative covenants close to the company's planned performance levels in order to keep pressure on the company's management to achieve the planned business targets.

The bank(s) also will make it clear to the management that the company is being run for the banks' benefit. Management will be allowed little latitude in making major business decisions until the crisis has passed and the company's loans have been repaid.

Conclusion

Bank lending is a risky business for both the bank and the borrower. The bank takes on a credit-risk exposure to its customer. The borrower must consider various risks, in particular:

- the consequences of arranging an unsuitable loan structure
- the implications of any covenants in the loan agreement, and
- the possibility of eventually having to seek refinancing.

The risks can be lessened by open negotiations and a good business relationship between the bank and the customer, with both parties working towards the customer's success.

Glossary

Amortizing Loan
Loan for which the principal is repaid gradually over the term to maturity.

Assignment
Sale of loan rights from one bank to another.

Balloon Repayment Loan
Loan for which some of the principal is repaid gradually during its term, but most is repaid at maturity.

Banker's Acceptance Facility
Facility whereby a bank agrees to accept bills drawn on it by a customer, up to an agreed credit limit.

Base Rate
The benchmark rate of interest in the UK against which much bank borrowing and deposit rates are priced, particularly for individuals and smaller companies.

An administered rate set by each bank; base rate changes normally follow significant changes in three-month LIBOR.

Basis Point
One hundredth of 1% (0.01%); therefore 100 basis points = 1%.

Bullet Repayment Loan
Loan for which the principal is repaid in a lump sum at maturity.

Coupon Swap
An interest-rate swap in which the parties swap fixed for floating-rate payments. Also called a fixed/floating swap.

Covenant
Written undertaking by a borrower to comply with a condition of lending. Breach of a covenant will be an event of default.

Cross-Default Clause
Covenant in a loan agreement whereby an event of default will occur if the borrower defaults on any other loan.

Event of Default
Event that makes a borrower in default on a loan agreement, giving the bank the right to accelerate the loan repayment, i.e. call in the loan. Events of default are specified in the loan agreement and will include non-payment and breach of a covenant.

Evergreen
Open-ended bank facility with no fixed term. Regularly renewed, and until canceled by the bank, can continue indefinitely.

Frozen GAAP
See GAAP.

GAAP
Generally accepted accounting practise. Financial covenants apply the GAAP that currently applies (rolling GAAP) or the GAAP that applied at the time a loan agreement was made (frozen GAAP).

Gearing-Ratio Covenant
Covenant in which a borrower undertakes that its financial gearing ratio will not exceed a stated amount.

Grace Period
Period of time between a loan payment becoming overdue and the time when the bank has the right to take action for the event of default.

Typically a grace period might be three to ten days, giving the borrower time to rectify the problem.

Guarantee
Undertaking by a third party, such as the parent company of the borrower, to meet any unpaid loan obligations of the borrower, in an event of default.

Interest-Cover Test
Covenant in which a borrower undertakes that the ratio of its profits, before interest and tax, to its interest costs will not fall below a stated level.

Junior Debt
Unsecured loan ranking behind senior debt in rights to payment in the event of the borrower's liquidation.

Letter of Comfort
Letter from a parent company to a bank on behalf of a subsidiary. The parent company undertakes to ensure, if it can, that subsidiary will honor its debt-payment obligations to the bank.

LIBOR
London Interbank Offered Rate. Theoretically the rate in the interbank money market at which a prime bank (a bank with a high credit rating) will lend to another prime bank.

Material Adverse-Change Clause
Covenant in a loan agreement whereby an event of default will occur if the bank judges that a significant change has taken place for the worse in the borrower's business or financial position.

Mortgage Loan
Amortizing loan secured against property.

Multiple-Option Facility
Facility provided by a syndicate of banks under which the borrower can choose to draw down funds in a variety of ways.

Negative Pledge
Covenant whereby a borrower promises that it will not create any new creditor ranking ahead of the lender in seniority, i.e. in the right to repayment in the event of liquidation of the borrower's business.

Novation
Transfer of a loan or part of a loan from one bank to another. A direct lending relationship is established between the new lender and the borrower. In this respect, novation differs from sub-participation.

Off-Balance-Sheet Transactions
Transactions that are not shown on a company's balance sheet. In the case of banks, these include undrawn facilities, letters of credit, guarantees and bonds.

Refinancing
Obtaining new finance to replace maturing loans, or renegotiating loans when the borrower is in default, or expects to become in default, on existing loans.

Representations
A statement made by a would-be borrower to the bank, giving details about the borrower or its circumstances. A bank will use the information given in representations to decide whether to lend, and if so on what terms. Representations may be written into the loan agreement as conditions or warranties.

Revolving Facility
Bank-lending facility whereby funds can be repeatedly borrowed, repaid, and then reborrowed at any time up to the limit of the facility.

Risk-Weighted Asset
See Weighted-Risk Asset.

Rolling GAAP
See GAAP.

Sawtooth Repayment
Irregular pattern for the repayment of loan principal over the term to maturity.

Secondary-Loan Sale
Transfer (novation), assignment or sub-participation of a loan.

Securitization
Process of packaging loans and other debts such as mortgages and trade debtors, into securities for sale to investors.

Senior Debt
Loan ranking ahead of other creditors in a liquidation.

Silent Participation
Sub-participation in a loan without the borrower's knowledge.

Subordinate Debt
Debt that ranks behind senior debt in a liquidation, but ahead of the equity.

Sub-Participation
Transfer of part of a loan from one bank to another. The borrower's lending relationship is with the original lending bank only, and not with the sub-participating bank. The sub-participating bank lends to the original lending bank. In this respect, participation differs from novation.

Swap
An agreement between two parties to exchange a series of future payments. In an interest-rate swap, the exchange of payments is from payments on one interest-rate basis, e.g. a fixed rate, to payments on another interest-rate basis, e.g. six-month LIBOR.

Syndicated loan
Loan agreement in which a borrower arranges to borrow money from a number of different banks, but with just one loan agreement. The lending banks are referred to as the syndicate.

Term Sheet
A document setting out the broad terms of a loan or facility agreement. Drawn up by the bank for the borrower to agree. Not a legally binding document.

Warranty
Confirmation by a borrower that certain information provided as a precondition of lending is correct. Breach of a warranty will not be an event of default, but might give the bank a right to take legal action against the borrower.

Weighted-Risk Asset
An asset of a bank, valued according to the risk that the asset will suffer a loss or fall in value. Assets are given different-value weightings from 0% to 100% according to the degree of risk. Also called Risk-Weighted Asset.

Withholding Tax
Tax deducted at source. In the case of a loan, the borrower deducts withholding tax on payments of interest, and the lender or investor receives interest net of tax. Withholding tax usually is recoverable at a later time.

Index